THE
SWITCH

The  Report

Love great sportswriting? So do we.

Every month, Pitch Publishing brings together the best of our world through our monthly newsletter — a space for readers, writers and fans to connect over the books, people and moments that make sport so captivating.

You'll find previews of new releases, extracts from our latest titles, behind-the-scenes interviews with authors and the occasional giveaway or competition thrown in for good measure.

We also dip into our back catalogue to unearth forgotten gems and celebrate timeless tales that shaped sporting culture.

Scan the **QR code** and join the growing Pitch Publishing reader community today.

THE SWITCH

FROM 24 STONE TO A LEAN, ULTRA RUNNING BOXER

KYLE CONWAY

First published by Pitch Publishing, 2026

Pitch Publishing
9 Donnington Park, 85 Birdham Road
Chichester, West Sussex, PO20 7AJ
www.pitchpublishing.co.uk
info@pitchpublishing.co.uk

© 2026, Kyle Conway

The moral right of the author and illustrator has been asserted in accordance with the Copyright, Designs and Patents Act 1988

Every effort has been made to trace the copyright.
Any oversight will be rectified in future editions at the earliest opportunity by the publisher.

No part of this book may be used or reproduced in any manner for the purpose of training artificial intelligence technologies or systems. In accordance with Article 4(3) of the DSM Directive 2019/790, Pitch Publishing expressly reserves this work from the text and data mining exception.

Set in Minion Pro 11.2/16.5pt

Typeset by Pitch Publishing

Jacket design by Gary Nickolls

Printed and bound by CPI Group (UK) Ltd, Croydon, CR0 4YY

The authorised representative in the EEA is
Easy Access System Europe OÜ, Mustamäe tee 50, 10621 Tallinn, Estonia gpsr.requests@easproject.com

A CIP catalogue record for this book is available from the British Library

ISBN 978 1 83680 226 6

Papers used by Pitch Publishing are from well-managed forests and other responsible sources

Contents

1. The Switch 9
2. Origin Story 23
3. Mallorca Here I Come 36
4. Portsmouth 46
5. Alone 64
6. Help 84
7. Road to Ultra 100
8. Can I Call Myself an Ultra-runner? 113
9. Running into the Future 134
10. Running into the Future, Part 2 151
11. New Year, New Me! 160
12. On your Bike 181
13. A Shot at Redemption! 191
14. Back to Running 207
15. It All Makes Sense Now 221
16. Where Am I Now? 242

Acknowledgements 251

To my loving wife. This book is as much yours as it is mine; without you these pages would be empty.

Chapter 1
The Switch

I WAS sweating and I felt bloated. We'd had a few drinks and had eaten. I ate a lot as usual. Even though I knew it wasn't a good idea, and I wasn't hungry any more, I still ate all the Chinese I had ordered and I gobbled down everything the kids hadn't managed to finish.

Now we sat on Simon's sofa. His sofa is one of those big, soft corner sofas that you can just sink into and not move for hours. Despite the comfy sofa, I was in pain. My stomach felt like it was going to pop. I wanted to take my trousers off, but that wouldn't have been appropriate in front of the kids and Simon's wife Kaylee: she might get the wrong idea. I didn't want anyone getting an unwarranted eyeful of my stomach or anything else for that matter.

Along with my physical discomfort, I was in mental turmoil. My anxiety was in overdrive. I really didn't want to see myself in the wedding videos that

Simon had invited us round to view. This was the first showing of his and Kaylee's wedding videos. The ceremony had been in August 2019, and I had the honour of being best man, and now it was December. As I sat in his living room with the wives and children, I had an overwhelming urge to get out of the house.

I can't explain how much effort it took to stop myself from creating an excuse and running away. I couldn't decide which was more embarrassing: me obviously creating a fake emergency to leave, or watching myself on screen. I decided to stay, and if it got that bad, I could close my eyes. Anyway, if I did attempt to run out of the house, I might have had a heart attack, but most probably my current physical situation would have seen me only move a few steps before violently vomiting a vast amount of Chinese food all over the kids.

The reason I was anxious about seeing the recording from the wedding is that I had major issues with my self-image. Over the previous few years I had let myself go and ballooned up in weight to over 24 stone. I hated the way I looked. I couldn't even look at myself in a mirror, never mind spending the next few hours seeing myself in someone's videos and pictures. It made me physically sick (although that could have been the takeaway) and despite the comfortable sofa, I became fidgety and sweaty.

Of course, I did the 'macho' thing, and I hid these feelings from the people around me in the room, even though they were the people who loved and cared for me the most. I sadly remember thinking how embarrassed Simon and Kaylee must be to have me in their wedding videos. I remember feeling that my beautiful wife, Charlotte, must also feel embarrassed to be with me, and I felt incredible shame that I was setting a bad example to my two children, Chloe and Archie. I also couldn't reason in my mind why these people, my family, and friends, would even bother with someone like me.

This is how bad it had become for me at that time in my life, and I can see how incredibly selfish that may seem now.

As I was sitting there fidgety and sweaty, in a pit of equal amounts of anxiety and embarrassment, Simon, being one of the two people that know me better than I do myself, must have realised I was in some sort of turmoil. He asked if I was okay and commented on my sweaty forehead. 'Bigman! What's up with you? Are you hot? You're sweating.'

'Yeah, I am fine; it's that shredded chilli beef, it's doing a number on me,' I lied. He laughed at this and grabbed me another cherry-flavoured beer that he became a walking advert for. To be fair, they were quite nice.

A few things to mention at this point. Number one, my closest group of friends all call me Bigman, and have done for years since we were young. At this time, I was standing at 6ft 4in and over 24 stone. I can't blame them really; when I look back over the years, I have always been taller and wider than them at every age.

It's a strange nickname because it gives me two feelings, depending on how much booze I have drunk. The first feeling is when we have had a few drinks; it makes me feel important, it inflates my ego. It makes me feel, 'Yeah, I'm the Bigman, the boss man, and I can drink more than anyone.' When I say I could drink more than anyone, that is of course a lie, but it didn't stop me trying; my party trick was to drink a pint with no hand by picking the glass up with my teeth and gulping it down in seconds without spilling a drop.

Then the second feeling comes when I am completely sober. Then I know that no one sees it the way I do after I have had a skinful. When I am drunk, my confidence is temporarily inflated, and it's easier to lie to myself. When I am sober, I know I'm called Bigman because I am fat, and that stings sometimes. It especially stings when my wife and kids call me Bigman. My two best friends, Simon and Rob, and I spend a lot of time together as a group with our families. Si and Rob call me Bigman, so all the kids do, and then all the wives follow suit. Luckily, my wife tends to only call me Bigman when we are with the others; obviously, she calls me it in the bedroom, but that's for different reasons, I wish.

The other thing to mention is that, as soon as I had blamed the chilli beef for my strange behaviour, I thought I could have said I didn't feel well and left. I remember berating myself; in my head, I said I could have lied to get out of this situation. Unfortunately, this type of thought had become quite common. A few years before, I had started to invent excuses to get out of things where my body would be on show, or where I would feel uncomfortable with my weight.

One excuse I used was that I was allergic to chlorine, so I would not have to go swimming with family and friends. My embarrassment about my body was so bad that I used this excuse not to take my kids swimming. It wasn't because I didn't want to play in the pool with them or teach them to swim; it was because this feeling of shame paralysed me. I physically couldn't take my top off in front of anyone – I felt *that* uncomfortable. Unfortunately, my family still think I am allergic to chlorine, so as they read this, I hope they can forgive me and understand just a little why I said it.

So, the time had come. Kaylee and Charlotte had all the kids sitting down, ready to watch the wedding videos. They were excited to see themselves dressed up. I wish I could have matched their excitement, but I couldn't. The familiar feeling of dread built up. Simon pressed play on the first video. It came as a relief that it was just a recording of the bride and bridesmaids getting ready in the morning. The next one was a scenic shot of people gathering outside the wedding venue.

Then, suddenly, the camera panned to the left, and there I was standing next to Simon in our wedding suits. I was handing him a cheeky shot of whisky from my hip flask, which I had smuggled into the venue. Everyone in the vicinity was laughing at us being caught out having a crafty shot. However, all I could think about was how big I looked compared to everyone else in their wedding finery. I could also see that I was sweating. The sun's rays were visibly glistening on the beading droplets on my forehead as we stood in a stunning vineyard waiting for the bride. This caused another stab of shame and self-loathing.

As we sat there watching, I also felt self-conscious about the best man's suit that I was wearing. I had flashbacks to the suit fittings for the groomsmen; it was clear that the clothes Simon wanted for his wedding were not going to fit me. Everyone had all their suits and trousers on in the tailor's, doing spins and checking themselves in the mirror, and rightly so, the handsome buggers. I sat there watching. I had the thought running through my head that I might be asked not to be best man anymore because the suits they were wearing didn't fit and they didn't have any in my size.

I saw Simon talking quietly to the tailor while I sat there watching. Simon walked over to me, and I couldn't help but think, 'This is where I get demoted from best man.' However, with a smile on his face, he told me that he was going to have to get my waistcoat and jacket specially made. Bless him, he didn't seem to be bothered at all by the fact he had to do this, but I had a massive problem with it. Simon was having to pay extra money out of his wedding fund because of me and how I struggled to control myself around a buffet, or in a sweet shop, or in a pub. However, I loved him for the way that it wasn't even a problem for him to do this, and I always will. Just writing this on paper at this point in my life, I feel a mix of gratitude and love for Simon with a lining of guilt that he had to do that for me.

There were a few more videos that were played where I featured only in small parts. In many I could be seen in the background eating or drinking. Then we got to the speeches. This was what I was really dreading – watching myself talk and having everyone's focus on me. I really didn't want to see myself, I didn't want to see my face and I didn't want to hear my voice. More importantly, I didn't want anyone else to either.

I remember the speech I gave very well. I had been worried all day, and I needed to have a few drinks to get up the courage to stand and talk in front of a room full of people in their wedding finery. The expectation for me to make them laugh was massive. To be honest, when you go to a wedding of someone you know very well, a family member or a good friend, the best man's speech is the highlight of the day. It's the only reason why some people go to weddings: it is for me anyway. I think a best man's speech signifies the time when all the serious stuff is done and it's now time to drink and be merry.

I had managed to get to that nice point of intoxication where your confidence goes through the roof, but you are still 95 per cent in control of yourself and your bodily functions. I remember standing there and people laughing at the jokes I had written; I remember handing around several compromising photos of Simon in stages of drunkenness and undress; I handed a picture of Simon's arse to his new in-laws. Hopefully that was the first time they had seen it. When I was giving the speech with my false confidence derived from alcohol, it felt good, I felt good.

However, it wasn't good to watch the whole thing back from where I was now sitting. Probably because

I wasn't drunk. I don't think many people really enjoy watching or hearing themselves talk. A recording of your own voice always sounds different from the voice in your head. While we all watched and the people sitting around me laughed, all I could think was that I looked massive. For some reason, I had the peculiar thought that my arms looked too small for my round body. To me, it looked odd, like when you stick twigs into a snowman's body for arms, old Kyle twig-arms.

The worst thing was that I had the feeling the people who were watching this with me weren't laughing at what I was saying, but they were laughing at the way I looked. They were laughing and commenting on what I was saying, and all I could do was smile along with them and pretend I was enjoying it as much as they were. I stood up and went to the fridge to get some beers, just to have a short respite from watching the videos.

To be honest, that wasn't even the worst video of me by far; the worst one came as a surprise. It had been filmed later in the night after the speeches and the lovely food, a short while after the evening guests had arrived. I was on the dance floor with Simon and Rob; all three of us by this point were quite intoxicated. The video showed the three of us dancing. By this point we had taken our jackets and waistcoats off. I was the only one sweating profusely, my white wedding shirt had become see-through, and I could see the shape of my body through the shirt.

At one point in the video, I raised my hand in the air, which pulled my shirt up, and I could see my stomach hanging over my trousers. I then attempted a graceful spin only to greet the camera with my sweaty arse crack peeking over my trousers. The room was laughing again, and this time, they were definitely all laughing at me. I was mortified to see this, and a feeling of overwhelming frustration and anger rose up in me. It was the type of frustration that made your hands go numb: the type that makes you want to cry and go home because there is literally nothing you can do. I wanted to leave that room so badly. I wanted to get away from everyone, but most of all I wanted to get away from myself. I went to the toilet and then grabbed some water.

When I came back, a strange thing happened while we watched the videos. I sort of went in on myself and stopped talking. I went into my own head. I had the feeling that I wasn't really there in the room. I stopped watching the videos, even though I was still staring at the TV. I wasn't taking anything in. I just sat in silence, sipping yet another cherry beer. It's strange because I had never gone in on myself like that before and haven't since. I now wonder if this was some sort of trauma response that people go into to protect themselves from further pain.

As I sat in silence, I started to talk to myself in my head. I asked myself: 'Why don't you leave the room?' I answered: 'Then everyone will know how you are feeling.' 'Why don't you want them to know?' This question was the hardest to answer, and I mused on it for the rest of the night. I knew I had the answer, but I couldn't quite put my finger on it. What was the problem with my family and best friend knowing how I felt about myself?

The night carried on and we had more drinks, but after a while, I stopped. For one of the first times in my life, I didn't feel like getting drunk anymore. I just wanted to be alone to answer the questions I had begun to ask myself. It kept going around in my head: 'Why don't you want them to know? Is it that it will make you feel weak?' No, that wasn't it.

Kaylee interrupted my thought: 'Bigman, you okay?'

'I'm absolutely knackered,' I lied. I turned to Charlotte and said, 'We will have to make a move in a minute as I need to get to bed.' Simon looked slightly sad as I think he had a later night planned. He had a new blow-up hot tub and wanted us to have a go with a nice glass of whisky. I couldn't think of anything worse, and I'm allergic to chlorine, remember.

Driving home, Charlotte looked across from the driver's side and asked if I was okay. 'You've gone quiet,' she said.

'I'm just tired.' That question was still going through my head as I sat in the passenger seat. We got home and got sorted for bed. I changed into some shorts and a t-shirt, avoiding the mirrors in the bedroom as usual. We got into bed and said our goodnights. There was no way I could sleep. I was mentally wired. I kept going over the night in my head like a video on repeat. I went over what I should have said or what I should have done to get out of the situation. I thought about what I should have done to avoid watching the wedding videos in the first place. Then, out of the blue, I thought: 'You don't want them to know because you would be admitting you aren't well.' And when you are not well you have to do something about it.

This realisation was as if someone had flicked a switch and a light bulb had gone on in my head. I knew I wasn't well mentally. What I had put myself through tonight wasn't normal, it wasn't healthy. Why was I doing this? The biggest driver must be my physical health and the fact I hated the way I looked. I lay there in bed in my semi-drunk and newly enlightened state. I made a promise to myself. I would never let myself feel this way again, especially the way I felt while watching those wedding videos. I was going to fix my issues. This promise seemed to be enough for my mind to give in and I dropped off to sleep not long after.

In the morning, I woke with a terrible hangover. I didn't realise how drunk I had been. As I lay there, I could remember everything that had been in my head before I fell asleep. I could feel the residual mental pain from the night before. I still had the realisation that I needed to change everything. Charlotte interrupted my thoughts and asked if I wanted a McDonald's breakfast, some grease to soak up the alcohol. To my surprise, I didn't want one. And, more to Charlotte's surprise, I said no.

For the rest of that day, I scoured the internet for diet plans, exercise plans, and any quick fixes to get me to lose weight. There was so much information and so many people all over the internet saying, 'This is the only way to get fit' and 'You have to eat this to be healthy.' I was confused. I watched videos of fit people saying diet is the best way. I read people's comments saying weight and strength training is the best way. I listened to people saying cardio is what you need to do to lose the most weight. I didn't know what I was going to do. There was so much to choose from. But I knew I was going to do something.

Looking back on this point of my life, I find it very difficult to talk about even now. I can now see I found it difficult at the time to admit I was not well both mentally and physically. I hated the way I looked and felt. I avoided mirrors and photo opportunities, so I didn't have to see myself or my reflection. I now know I did this as I found it easier to avoid the issues than face them head on. That night at Simon and Kaylee's forced me to ask myself some difficult questions. When I was able to answer them all, I could only repeat that it really was as if a switch had gone on in my brain. Like when you're standing in a dark room and flip the switch and you can suddenly see where you are.

I know it sounds cheesy, and experts say that to change a mindset takes time. They say it happens gradually, but it didn't for me. The switch was flicked, and, at the age of 32, I was going to change. I knew it was going to be the start of my journey to a better me.

To this day no one has known I felt this way, not even Charlotte or my best friends. I suppose they will now after reading this.

Chapter 2

Origin Story

I GREW up in a place called Longton, one of the six towns that make up the city of Stoke-on-Trent. I had a happy childhood. Well, what I can remember of it: my memory is shocking. I can't even remember what I had for dinner yesterday. Anyway, I grew up in a loving family. My dad left at an early age, and my mum worked hard to support and raise me. I spent a lot of time with my nan and grandad. My nan kept a clean house, and my grandad worked hard as a pipefitter welder. These are the people who taught me a solid work ethic.

From an early age, I was a big lad. I was the tallest in my year going through the whole of school, and I was always chubby. Throughout my childhood, other children would find joy in reminding me of my size and call me hurtful names as children do. I can't remember this affecting me much at the time, but it must have had a subconscious impact for me to get to where I was later in life. Even as an adult I still remember some of the names. Children can be cruel, and they don't know the lasting impact of their words and actions.

The worst thing for me was when older children saw my size. I became a target for them, a challenge, someone to pick on. I remember playing out with a friend at the time called Josh. He was slightly younger than me, he went to a different school, and he was much shorter than me. I must have been about 12 at the time, and we were both sitting on a wall in front of a chemist. A friend of Josh's older brother came along; he must have been around 16. For some reason, he took an instant dislike to me and became aggressive. I could tell he was going to hit me from the way he was standing and moving. He started shouting at me, 'Who do you think you are?' He grabbed me by the shoulders and pulled me off the wall. Just as he was about to give me a good hiding, I closed my eyes ready for impact.

None came. I had been saved by Josh's older brother. He rode up on his bike at just the right time and told the lad to leave me alone. Josh's brother told the lad my age, and he wouldn't believe it. Every time I saw him from that point, he tried to intimidate me, but he never got physical again. When I got a little older and bigger, I got some grit in me and started to challenge him back. When he was about 20 and I was 16, he was terrified of me.

In my early life, my two cousins Ash and Asa were born. Now there were three of us and my nan looked after us all. Luckily, I can remember long summer holidays playing in my nan and grandad's large back garden. We would spend our days climbing trees and making bows and arrows out of old wood and garden canes. Looking back, I am not sure how none of us got seriously hurt. These bows and arrows were deadly weapons and would easily pierce skin.

I remember one summer we were on the garage roof; we would like to sit there and survey the land and trees. On this particular day, I decided it would be a good idea to jump across on the neighbour's garage and then on to his porch roof. I steadied my nerves. I told Ash to count to three, and then I dashed across. Jumping like a cat from one roof to another, I had made it all the way across, great success. I then had to quickly turn around and go before anyone in the street saw me. On the return trip, I heard a loud crack, and I suddenly felt myself falling. Everything went into slow motion. I had only gone and fallen through the neighbour's garage roof. My weight had split the asbestos tiles, and I hit the deck hard.

Events were no longer in slow motion. When the realisation of what I had done hit me, time sped up. I immediately jumped up and managed to pull myself out of the garage through the hole I had created. Unhurt, other than a bruised arse, I had to report to my nan what I had done. I was terrified. Ash was also scared and hid in the trees. He thought he would get into trouble too. To my surprise, there was no shouting or telling me off, there was only concern. The thing I feared most was having to tell my grandad when he got home from work.

I sat in the garden with a horrible, knotted, sickly feeling in my gut for a good few hours, waiting for him. When he got home, I told him. Again, I was pleasantly surprised, no smack, no shouting. I thought this was the worst thing I had ever done in my life, and I expected a bollocking. Again, none came: there was only concern. My grandad went next door, and with the neighbour, assessed the damage. Thankfully, there was no car in the garage. I then sat waiting for him to come back, but they both called me over into the garage.

I thought: 'This is where I will get my bollocking,' but no. All they did was question me on how I got out after I got in. I told them I put my foot on the bracket on the wall and then jumped up and pulled myself out through the hole. There was no bracket on the wall, and they were stumped as to how I'd got out. According to them, it was impossible for me to have jumped out. It left them perplexed, but me mostly because I can see it clearly in my mind. There was a metal bracket, the sort that holds a ladder, and in my terror, I put my foot on it and leapt up and pulled myself out. To be fair, they could have removed the bracket because I bent it or something; they were always winding us kids up.

As a young lad of my size, my family tried to help me lose weight. I was murder with chocolates and sweets; I would sneak chocolates and biscuits out of the treat cupboard. Rather than one brownie, I would eat two. I kept this practice up for most of my life.

My mum tried to get me into jiu-jitsu. I kept doing it for a while and got a few belts. I would do back-to-back competitions where two people would kneel back-to-back and then grapple to pin the other down. Due to my size and weight, I got really good, and then they started to put me up against older boys, and I was beating them too. Then one day they put me against one of the teen girls, and she wiped the floor with me; she absolutely destroyed me. It didn't help that I fancied the pants off her. This loss rocked my confidence, and the other boys would hound me for losing to a girl. The thing that annoys me now is that she would have wiped the floor with them also. In the end, I just stopped going. I often wonder what would have happened if I had ignored them and kept doing the back-to-back competitions.

My grandad had been a great goalkeeper back in his day, and he tried to get me into that. I played a few games for a team his friend coached, and I hated every second of it. I think in my first match I let five goals in. I hung up my boots and quit immediately. Then in high school, two teachers encouraged me to play rugby. I loved it. In this sport, my size and weight were actually useful, and I began to gain confidence the better I played. I started to play for a team outside of school and we travelled all over the Midlands playing other teams. It was nice to have team-mates who looked after each other. If anyone kicked off on the pitch, I knew my team-mates would be there to get my back. Playing rugby gave me the confidence to stand up for myself and fight back against the children who called me names and the older ones who saw me as an easy target.

As I got older, I started to hang around with my friends rather than going to my nan's house. It was great. My mum worked full-time, so it was just me and the lads every summer and school holidays. We got up to some mischief and had some adventures. We explored the surrounding countryside, camping and setting fires, and all the old, abandoned factories left behind by the decline of the pottery industry for which Stoke was famous.

I enjoyed this part of my childhood, but as I got to the age of 14 or 15, my view of where I lived started to change. I moved into a phase of life where alcohol, drugs and violence became more prevalent. My high school was terrible for violence. I saw a boy get stabbed in the shoulder, and the person who did it said: 'It's a good job he moved, because I was aiming for his head.' Fighting was commonplace, as were drugs.

The city was struggling with the decline of its main industry, and many of its hard-working people were out of jobs. Some turned to drugs and the heart of the city was gone. It became common for us to see used needles on the floor outside the school gates. This was the time I began to fantasise about leaving the Potteries behind, and England altogether.

When I reached 16, I looked old enough to get into pubs and clubs and began to sample the nightlife of Hanley, another of the six towns. I also began to work in a youth centre, so I was getting some good money coming in for someone that was 16 years of age and still living with mummy. Around this age, I stopped playing rugby as the going out, booze and girls became more attractive to me. I slowly started putting weight on from the drinking and lack of exercise, but I had a good set of friends. Simon, Rob and I were the backbone of the group.

By the time I was 17, I was 17 stone. I had a steady girlfriend at the time, and I was still thinking about leaving England, but not doing anything about it. I sadly found out my girlfriend was cheating on me with a close friend. This pushed me to make the best decision of my life. I applied for a job with a place called the Holiday Soccer School. It was run by a large holiday firm, and they were looking for coaches to deliver football sessions to young people all over Europe as part of a package holiday. I got called to a two-day group interview in a holiday park on the east coast.

Just before I left for the group interview, I had my 18th birthday, and it was a good one. A friend and I went drinking in the clubs in Stoke. In the morning, I woke up completely naked, which was unusual as even at my drunkest I wouldn't sleep without a t-shirt on in case someone saw my body. In my wardrobe was a full-length mirror; as I opened it to get a clean shirt, I caught an image of myself. This is where I got a good taste of self-disgust. Even then I thought I looked horrible.

I quickly got dressed and went to the bathroom. In there I saw my mum's scales. I hopped on and closed my eyes. When I opened them, I was over 18 stone: I was 18 years old, and over 18 stone. That's over one stone for every year of my life. Even back then I knew I wasn't in good shape, and I had real body image issues.

When I arrived at the multi-day interview, I instantly felt out of place. I was surrounded by young, sleek football players who had proper skills, and here I was, a 6ft 4in, 18-stone ex-rugby player who didn't really like football or know the rules. All I kept telling myself was 'Don't mess it up, this is your opportunity to get away from England.'

We did a load of team activities and tests, and then on the final day we had individual interviews with the heads of the school. We would be told that we were going to be employed and where in the world we were going, or we would be getting the bad news: sorry, try again next year. I remember being given an early time for my interview and thinking: 'That's a bad sign. They will want to get rid of all the "Sorry but no thanks" people first.'

I walked into a lobby area and saw some of the other lads already waiting there, nervous looks plastered on their faces, and I wondered why they were already there: their interviews were after mine. I sat next to a lad called Paul, who recognised me from the activities the previous day. We started to chat about how we didn't think we would get through. Mid-sentence the door to the main hall opened, and an upset-looking guy came out. He seemed deflated, hunched over. He picked up a bag and quickly walked out without saying a word. Paul and I looked at each other, worry across our faces. I was just about to mention that worry to Paul when my name was called from the main hall doorway.

I was led into the entertainment hall. The two head honchos of the soccer school sat behind a table in the centre of the dance floor in front of the stage. I was asked to sit. The formality was new to me, and I struggled with it. They asked me about my youth work and how I came to get an FA Level 1 coaching certificate, which was entirely by luck and being in the right place at the right time, but I didn't tell them that. (I had been working with Stoke-on-Trent youth services on a project called Sport on the Court and I was one of the project workers. The council paid for a few of us to do our Level 1 football, and a tennis qualification.) They asked me a few more questions about why I wanted to work overseas in holiday resorts. I replied with some generic job interview stuff I had memorised from the internet. They told me the interview was over, and it went silent.

I sat there staring at them. I held my breath until one of them, out of the blue, shot his hand directly out in front of him. I took a deep breath to stop myself passing out and looked at his hand for a moment. I must have looked as if I didn't understand a handshake. It eventually clicked. He wanted to shake my hand. I stood up, grabbed his hand and excitedly shook it, way too hard. He said 'Congratulations' and asked me to sit back down. He went on to explain that over the past two days they had been impressed with me and would like to offer me a position at their flagship school in Mallorca. This would give me the opportunity to train holidaymakers at Estadi Municipal Els Arcs, the stadium of UD Alcúdia football club, and was only offered to the highest-scoring candidates from the weekend's activities.

I sat there in a hazy cloud of pride. They said they would be in touch with flights and start dates and told me to go and celebrate. I accepted with glee. I couldn't believe it. I had my opportunity to get out of England. I walked out of the room and made my way to Paul. I wanted to tell him everything, but all I managed to say was 'I got the job,' and then he was called in. I thought about waiting for him, but my excitement took over. I grabbed my stuff and found a quiet place to call my mum; she was over the moon.

I made my way to the train station and started my journey back to Stoke. I was thinking about all the possibilities and fantasising about what life would be like living and working in Mallorca. A few stops and train changes went by in a blur until somewhere near Birmingham, Bez from the Happy Mondays got on the train and sat next to me. Everyone was staring at him; I didn't say anything to him other than 'Excuse me' as we rolled into Stoke because I was too busy dreaming of my new life in Mallorca.

For the next week, I told as many people as possible that I was out of there and didn't plan on being back. Everyone was happy for me. I eventually received my letters, start dates and plane tickets. They had only given me two weeks to prep. They had sent a list of what I should buy to take with me and a load of forms for me to fill in. I also had to get a doctor to sign me off. Two weeks didn't seem enough time to get it all sorted. I also had to inform work, who were not happy as my notice period was a month, but I wasn't going to let that stop me.

My friends were really happy for me. We had a big camping leaving party, around 20–25 people in a patch of woodland on the outskirts of Stoke with booze, music and tents. A big fire was lit, and we all sat around drinking and telling stories from the last time we were drunk. A few hours into the night, there were suddenly loads of torch lights and shouting. Two vanloads of police had shown up, and almost everyone scattered in different directions, but I and a few others just sat there.

The police let us pack up our stuff and walked us over to their vans. They asked us what we were doing. Simon, the least drunk, explained that it was my leaving do, and we were just camping. The police told us that they had had a call to say we were having an illegal rave. They had come to knock some heads but when they saw it was people camping, they were disappointed. They realised we might not all be of age; some of us were still to turn the big 18. It was a funny coincidence that everyone had forgotten their identification and where they lived. The police were actually a good laugh and gave us a lift to town and told us to go home. This left a good 15 people hiding in the woods all night thinking we had been arrested. Good times.

Leaving day came. I woke up early and checked my bags again, even though I had packed and triple-checked them the night before. Everything was in order. My mum made me a big breakfast, which I almost inhaled. I then loaded the car, and we set off to pick my nan up as she wanted to see me off too. We drove to Manchester airport. My nan and mum chatted away, but I sat in silence, wondering if this was the right decision. I told myself there was no backing out now. They kissed me goodbye, and I went through to check in. This didn't seem real. I was actually leaving and had no intention of coming back. I boarded a half-empty plane, stuck my headphones on, and wondered what was going to happen next.

Chapter 3

Mallorca Here I Come

I STEPPED off the plane into that familiar smell of runway, aviation fuel and heat that I loved as a child. To me it signified the start of a holiday, the start of an adventure. I walked through the strangely quiet Spanish airport. As it was two weeks before the early summer season started, there was hardly a holidaymaker in sight. I collected my bags while eyeing up the other people on my flight to see if I recognised any. Nope, not a single person from my initial interview.

I made my way out of the airport past the closed duty-free and many car-hire desks and found the person I was meant to meet. He was wearing a blue holiday rep top and held a clipboard. He told me we were in for a bit of a delay as we were waiting for another flight to come in. While we waited, the guy informed me that I was in for the best two weeks of my life. The next two weeks would be training and getting to know all the other staff, including the holiday reps, kids' reps, and entertainers. He told me that we got to go on all the trips that the company sold as extras so we had better sell them to guests.

Selling! I thought, 'No one told me about this.' The next words he said were, 'The football lads are lucky because they aren't required to sell anything.' What a relief. He then told me about the rep prices and discounts I would be eligible for at bars and clubs. It was music to my ears. The next two weeks would be a load of free trips and non-stop boozing.

The next plane landed, and I met the two room-mates that I would be working with at the soccer school. They were good lads but very different personality-wise. One was an ex-goalkeeper who had played a few games for a lower league club. His club released him, and he found himself in Mallorca. He loved to tell all the guests, especially the women, that he was a professional footballer. He was the type of guy that didn't have a hair on his head out of place. The other guy was unassuming and naïve. He took football coaching very seriously and I could tell he would be a stickler for the rules. We had yet to meet our boss, who would be arriving at a later date. My room-mates got the same lowdown as I had from our chaperone, and it was good to see they were both as excited as I was. We arrived at our base hotel, which was the company's flagship family resort on the island. We were told that we wouldn't be staying at the hotel, and that we had a flat down the road.

Unfortunately, the flat we walked into was a disgusting, cockroach-infested eyesore. The place only had two beds. I tried to lighten the mood and joked that they had best not sleep naked. We went back to the hotel and had to wait for the area director to come back. Apparently, they had not realised the state of the flat they had assigned to us. More worrying is that it had been advertised as a three-bedroom property but they hadn't checked the place before paying for it.

The director said they would upgrade us and gave us some new keys and a new address and sent us on our way. We got to our new flat, and it was clearly 100 per cent better from the outside. The building was a modern three-storey set of six flats with balconies, the cool type you see in Ibiza. As we lugged our bags to the ground floor flat, three ladies came down the stairs laughing and joking. To our young minds, each and every one of them was a stone-cold fox.

We all said our hellos, and it turned out they were kids' reps and entertainers. They had been there a night already and invited us to a big night out that very night. The big night out was where all the reps and session staff went out and got drunk. They call it team bonding. The three of us walked to the shop to get some beers and food to take back and got ready. Luckily, I had brought my CD player and some speakers because no one else had.

As we got ready, we heard the girls come back, and our conversation turned to which one we were going to try and pull, as you can imagine that three young men would who were full of bravado and confidence, and working away from home for the first time.

We were picked up in a taxi and taken to our first bar, and it was packed. These were the people I was going to work with for the summer season. Most people were on their first season, but there were some who had been there for a few. The veterans took the lead and showed us newbies the ropes. Over drinks, they told us what to expect and how to handle the holiday-makers. After the formalities, they led the drinking games. During the night, more and more people turned up, so that finally there must have been hundreds of us. I ended up talking to all sorts of people: kids' reps, office staff, main hotel reps and entertainers from all over the UK.

We then made our way to a large nightclub-type bar. It was in this bar that I was approached by one of the ladies that we had met when moving into the flat. Her name was Charlotte. I was instantly smitten. She was beautiful, chatty and really funny. I obviously challenged her to downing a local drink called a dog's bollocks. She took up the challenge and I wiped the floor with her. It was embarrassing for her, really! I forgave her for her failed attempt, the night went on and one thing led to another.

The next day, I woke up next to Charlotte in her flat, and for the life of me, I couldn't remember her name. I had to sneak out and back to my flat and ask my roomies what her name was. She's probably not going to be happy I told you this story: sorry, Charlotte. Anyway, over the next two weeks, I pitched woo at Charlotte. We attended all the mandatory excursions and drinking events together. We saw and did some spectacular things. We even spent a few hours chatting with a guy that came third in that year's *Big Brother*. I look back on those two weeks fondly, spending all that time with good people and meeting the woman I would eventually marry.

That fortnight was very much a honeymoon period with the job. Once we met our new boss and got into work, it became very difficult. We were up early and got to bed late, seven days a week. We were training and playing football in the heat of the day, then entertaining and promoting in the cooler hours. Once we got back to the flat, we would grab a bite to eat and hit the bars.

This lifestyle took its toll. I hardly ever got a rest and felt washed out. I knew I wasn't going to do the whole summer. The only thing keeping me there was Charlotte and the social life. Eventually, even Charlotte's allure couldn't keep me getting bossed about in the sweltering heat. One day, my boss was driving us back to the flat in the early evening. We had just herded hundreds of sugared-up, excited British kids around Alcúdia stadium. As I sat there my head jerked forward and I heard a crunch. The boss man had crashed the car.

It was only a small bump into the back of another driver, but you could tell it knocked his confidence. It was clear he was embarrassed. The other driver didn't even care, he just drove away. My two roomies and I were having a good laugh about it, but the boss man had a strange outburst and told us to shut up. That little crash must have had a big effect on him. After his outburst, the relationship went downhill. It was time to move on for me.

A few weeks later, I got my opportunity. A friend of mine called Steve emailed and asked if I fancied going to Germany for the football World Cup. He said we would camp at a backpacking place outside Berlin and travel to the fan zone every day. I had saved some cash, so I knew I could afford a few months bumming around in Europe. I told him to count me in. I promptly handed in my notice and then had a rather awkward conversation with Charlotte. It was sad, and I didn't want to leave her. We had recently dropped the love bombs and said we would make a go of the relationship. Now here I was telling her I was leaving to go and watch the World Cup in Germany. After several long nights of talking, we decided to try the long-distance thing and meet up in England when the summer season had finished. A few days later, I left Mallorca.

I got home to Stoke-on-Trent and spent a night at my mum's house, and the next day I was on a flight to Germany with my good friend Steve. We arrived at Schoenfeld airport near Berlin, and the place was buzzing with football fans from all over the world. We were eager to get to the campsite to drop our gear off and get out into the city. We managed to figure out the train system easily and then proceeded to get on one going in the wrong direction. Sheepishly, we got off at the next station and found the right train. Sitting on that train, I was wondering what Charlotte was up to in Mallorca. I told myself that I would send her a text later, letting her know I was safely in Germany.

We pulled up to our station. I looked out of the window, and the place seemed to be a quiet metropolitan town with tree-lined streets and not a single bit of litter. Everything seemed clean and uniform. I immediately thought that this was going to be a boring few weeks if we were staying here, but how wrong I was. We took a ten-minute walk out of the town only to find a massive old mansion which had been converted into a funky-looking travellers' hostel. It was surrounded by a few fields that had a scattering of tents in them. The place was amazing; it was full of all sorts of people from all over the world. There were football fans mixing with dreadlocked hippies that were mixing with office types in their chinos. It was a real melting pot.

Steve and I were slightly worried about what kind of reception we would get, a couple of English lads in the middle of Germany there to watch football. It could spell disaster, especially if we came across some football hooligans or people thought we were of the hooligan persuasion. However, we had no trouble at all. All I experienced on that trip was love from everyone we met. We didn't see or experience one ounce of trouble. It was amazing to be drinking with people from Brazil, Italy and Sweden all at the same time. I loved it.

One day we decided that we were going to chill at a lake nearby and swim rather than going to the city. Before leaving we were sitting around the fire in the morning eating chilli for breakfast. Steve was questioning me on Charlotte and what I was going to do. Were we going to stay together? Would a long-distance relationship work? It was almost like he was trying to get me to think negatively about long-distance relationships. To shut him up, I said I didn't know. We ate our delicious breakfast of chilli and cheese and set off for the lake. First, we had to stop off at a supermarket for beers. It was a pretty quiet walk to the supermarket because I was thinking of Charlotte and what Steve had been implying. We bought a crate of bottled beer and some bread for nourishment. Taking one handle of the beer crate each, we walked off towards the lake.

After around 30 minutes of walking, I said, 'Let's have a rest.' I sat on the grass with my back to a signpost and popped a beer open. My friend stayed stood in front of me and snapped a couple of photos of me. He slowly sat down next to me and asked what was up. I told him I was thinking about what he had said by the fire. He then showed me the photos he had just taken. I hadn't noticed, but I was leaning on the post of a massive sign that said Charlottenburg. He proceeded to tell me to get my head out of my arse and enjoy the trip. I took this as a sign from the universe and told myself I would give it a proper go with Charlotte. I also got my head out of my arse and enjoyed drinking beers at the lake.

Before leaving and returning to England, I spoke to Charlotte on the phone. She told me that she was going to return home at the end of the Mallorca season. A smile split across my face as I knew what she would say next. Charlotte asked if I would like to come down to Portsmouth and spend some time with her. I thought of the massive Charlottenburg sign and almost shouted out 'YES!' I wanted to see where this relationship went. I rang my mum and asked her to book a train ticket to Portsmouth for two weeks' time, which she did.

My friend and I remained in Germany and watched the World Cup Final at the fan zone by Brandenburg Gate. What an experience, to be at one of the biggest parties in the world – and I couldn't take it all in as I was too excited about seeing Charlotte. I just wanted to get back to England and travel down to the south coast. We flew home a couple of days later, and yet again I spent a short time at home, just enough for my mum to wash my clothes. Then I was back on that train heading off for a new adventure.

Chapter 4

Portsmouth

I STEPPED off the train at Havant, just outside Portsmouth. I was to be met by Charlotte's sister's boyfriend Neil. Charlotte was due to fly into London a few hours after my arrival on the south coast. Neil and I ended up doing a full pub crawl of Havant town centre and got to know each other. Rather tipsy, I got a text to say Charlotte was home and we made our way to Charlotte's dad's house. I walked through the door and was so happy to see Charlotte again. It was like we hadn't been apart. I met the rest of her family over a takeaway and a few more beers. The next day I was eagerly shown the sights of Portsmouth. I thought it was beautiful compared to Stoke-on-Trent. Charlotte lived two minutes from the beach and within driving distance of a couple of funfairs. We still got on like a house on fire and I was very much in love with her.

That night I told her I didn't want to leave. She suggested we move into a flat she owned with her sister and try living together. And that was the end of the story; I never went home. Well, that's not quite true. Charlotte bought a car, and we drove to my mum's to collect my belongings. I had another leaving bash, with all my friends and family. It must have been quite overwhelming for Charlotte to meet all my friends and family at the same time. She seemed to take it in her stride and got on with everyone. I was happy, and some of my mates were quite jealous – they thought she was fit. One of them said that I was punching way above my weight. I thought instantly that I wasn't sure how I could, as I was 18 stone.

After the gathering and the hangovers receded, we left for Portsmouth with a small car full of my belongings. We spent the next few days moving into the flat and popping to places like Ikea to buy rubbish coffee tables and lamps that never get switched on. I still had some money left, but it was quickly running out. Charlotte got a job no problem. She went back to her old nursery school as a manager. I think that this is where the wheels came off for me. I was looking for a job for a while and nothing came up. With Charlotte working every day, I got bored and lonely. I didn't have any friends down south; Charlotte's friends were great, but they were all working also. The fun and excitement of the back-to-back adventures had worn off. I slipped into drinking every night and eventually escalated into day drinking.

I was also eating junk while Charlotte was at work. I would drink nearly a crate of cider a day and eat crisps and chocolate for breakfast, lunch and dinner. I started to put on weight, and I was now over 19 stone. I spent my last few pounds on a gym membership, promising myself and Charlotte I would get in shape and get a job. I did neither, so it was a waste of money. I felt so alone. Charlotte could see something was up and one night sat me down. In the nicest possible way, she told me to get a job and sort myself out, or go home to my mum. I knew she was serious, so I cut my drinking out.

I didn't knock it on the head totally. I still drank socially but now not at 9am on a Tuesday morning while watching Jeremy Kyle. I got a job that involved early, late, night, weekend and holiday shifts all on a rota pattern. I was bringing in some money and not drinking. Charlotte was happy, but I started to feel I had a hole inside of me. I put it down to my new normal life. I now had a job, bills to pay and a partner. Next would be kids, a pet dog and a mortgage. That felt like a trap for life.

One evening, I was looking at new jobs in the paper and there was a story about a local rugby team. Reading the story took me back to my childhood with fond memories of playing rugby with my mates. I fired off an email to the club and was invited down to training. I was equal parts excited and nervous. I told Charlotte I wasn't going to go, but she knew it would be good for me. Under duress she took me to a sports shop, where I brought some boots, shorts and a gum shield.

A couple of days later, I rocked up at the club and immediately felt intimidated. There were loads of massive, scary-looking blokes all indulging in banter. I didn't know anyone, and I had seemed to have forgotten that I was also massive and scary at 6ft 4in and currently inching past 19 stone. My initial intimidations were short-lived as I trained with the third and fourth teams, not the supermen in the first team. This was definitely more my speed. I really enjoyed my first session and committed to attending the following week.

The day of the next session came, and again I didn't want to attend, and again Charlotte talked me into it. Without Charlotte forcing me to do stuff over the years, I would have become a hermit by now. The second session was awesome, and I loved the feeling of using my body again. I was invited to play in that weekend's game.

The Saturday of the game arrived and again nervousness hit me. I didn't want to be rubbish. I didn't want to let the team down. This time Charlotte didn't need to force me or talk me into anything. I just went. I remember starting the match. I was put in the team as a prop, the exact position I had played as a kid. We had kick-off and as soon as the whistle went, I ran directly towards where the ball was going to land. I was going as fast as I could, with the intent that whoever on the opposing team caught it was getting smashed. By the time I got to where the ball was, I was too out of breath to smash anyone. I immediately regretted sprinting for a full 30 seconds. With a stitch and gasping for breath, I thought to myself: 'Bugger, this is going to be a long game.'

Ten minutes in, I got a second wind and used it up straight away with a ten-second burst towards the try line. I thought my luck was in and I was about to score a try on my debut and cement myself as a legend in the team. However, I ran out of steam and was quickly set upon by the opposing forward pack. I lay on the floor for a while, trying to get my breath and strength back. I slowly dragged myself out of the mud and made a token effort at running to the next breakdown in the game.

Finally, the whistle went, and the game was over. I asked a team-mate if they knew the score. To my shock, we had lost about 60-0. I thought that this huge defeat would cause everyone to be angry or sad. I expected a frosty and quiet atmosphere in the changing room. How wrong was I? Someone put some loud music on. A crate of beer was brought out and bottles of port were passed around. Everyone was singing and drinking. I was invited out with the team on a social that night. I peeled myself out of my wet, muddy strip and had a shower. I joined the team in the bar for food. After several hours of drinking games and witnessing people drinking out of dirty rugby boots, normal rugby lad stuff, we all hit the town for some proper drinking.

I strolled through my front door at around 4am, drunk as a happy skunk. After a few hours' sleep I woke up with a sickening hangover and a mouth like I had been eating sand. But, worst of all, my muscles in my legs and shoulders were in the worst pain I had ever felt. I literally couldn't move.

Despite the agony my body was in after that one game and night out, I played rugby most weeks, work permitting. It began to fill that hole inside of me. I had found a good group of friends and looked forward to playing as often as I could. My weight at this time always hovered around 18–19 stone. I was training once a week and playing at the weekend, but I continued eating rubbish food and drinking alcohol. I used training and playing matches as an excuse to eat takeaways as a treat. I told myself, 'Kyle, you have trained hard and you have played hard, and you deserve a whole large pizza for dinner and a McDonald's breakfast in the morning.'

This went on for a few years; playing rugby and then using it as an excuse to eat crap became normal life for me. I made a token effort to lose some weight when my daughter Chloe was born in 2008. I was a dad now and felt the urge to better myself. But this didn't last long and the call of the junk food drew me back in.

Then in 2010 I got a little more serious about losing weight. It was the year I got married to the love of my life, Charlotte, and I wanted to look good for her on our big day. I wanted to give her a perfect wedding. I managed to lose some weight by hitting the gym and not eating as much junk. This lasted until 2011, when Archie, our son, was born. With two young children, a mortgage and a busy job to contend with, I went back to my old eating habits and stopped going to the gym. The hard work I did for the wedding was quickly erased and my weight went back up. I had that thought that I needed to do something but it was easy to ignore it. Charlotte and the kids never said anything, never mentioned my weight.

Despite being back to around 19 stone, I got better at playing rugby. I moved around the pitch more and wasn't as knackered after the match. One weekend in 2016 we had a big game against a local rival. I turned up to the clubhouse jittery on coffee and Red Bull. I wanted to get on the pitch and make some big hits. Just before half-time in the opposition half, I found myself late to a ruck as usual. I saw an opportunity to pick and go. I picked the ball up and set my focus on the try line. Smash! I barged my way over the opposition prop. I had a clear run to the try line.

In my head, I thought I looked the business. I felt like one of the all-time great props, like Joe Marler or Phil Vickery. In reality, I was a 19-stone muppet, quickly running out of breath. I was so quickly knackered, the opposition winger had time to get from one side of the pitch and tackle me, directly into my right knee just as I planted it on the floor. I felt the pain instantly and dropped to the turf as if a sniper had just shot me in the head. I managed to place the ball back like a professional, so my team still had a chance. The backs picked it up and then lost it to the opposition – typical backs.

I tried to stand up. As soon as I put weight on my knee, I was back on the floor. That was my game over. I hobbled into the changing rooms, and my knee was already swelling to a concerning size. I had a shower, watched the rest of the game, and had a few pints. I knew something must be really wrong when I could no longer get out of my chair at the bar. I quickly rang Charlotte, who dutifully picked me up and drove me to the hospital. I remember debating whether I should just go home or go to the hospital another day. It was the Six Nations and England were playing France, and I really didn't want to miss it.

Charlotte, however, made me go to the hospital. I went quickly through to see a doctor who happened to be a fellow rugby fan, although he did support Wales. He promptly sent me for an X-ray. During the X-ray, I knew the England match would have been well underway. When I came out of the X-ray room, the nurse pushing my wheelchair told me that my doctor had asked me to be put in this sub-waiting room-type place. There was no one else but me in it. On the wall was a TV, and she put the second half of the match on, which was really kind of her.

I wish I could remember the doctor's name; he was a legend for doing that. After the match, he reviewed my X-ray and said he couldn't really see what was wrong with the knee. He knew there was something wrong due to the swelling and pain. He sent me on my way with some crutches and an appointment to see a specialist a few days later. I spent the next few days enjoying being waited on hand and foot in front of the TV, eating rubbish.

I turned up to my appointment and met another rugby-loving doctor: this one was an England fan. He did some poking around and ordered me an MRI scan. He actually got me in that day. All I had to do was wait for three hours. It was lucky that the MRI was only for my leg because the radiologist told me that due to my size, I would not have fitted in his machine. I thought, 'Thanks, mate. Just do your job and scan me.' After the scan I was sent home and told I would get an appointment when the specialist had looked at my images.

I spent a few more days on the sofa eating and drinking. I got signed off from work, which was a bonus. I got a letter summoning me back to the hospital. I was taken into a waiting room with only one other person. I sat in there for nearly two hours past my original appointment time. I wasn't angry; I was just worried about how much Charlotte would have to pay for parking.

My specialist consultant came into the room and called my name. He apologised for being late and told me he had lost track of time. I didn't think that was a good sign, although for some reason I really liked the guy. He told me he had reviewed my MRI and that it was clear that I had torn my anterior cruciate ligament and there was some damage to my meniscus. He went on to say that I would need an operation to repair my ACL and have microfractures to make my bone bleed. The bleeding bone would form a new cushion between my thigh bone and lower leg bone, or it would be bone-on-bone action.

We discussed at great length what that meant for me. He told me that rugby would be off the cards. He was concerned with my weight and suggested it could destroy the new cushion created by the microfractures. He told me that losing weight would help. We discussed that if I lost weight and the microfractures worked I might be able to run short distances. I told him that I could barely run short distances as it was. Rather than laugh, he just ignored my failed attempt at a joke. I went home with some exercises to do, which I never did. I was told that an appointment for my operation would be sent shortly.

I got signed off from work and waited and waited and waited for my operation. I started to get bored again. I went to the clubhouse on a weekend to watch the match, but I got frustrated that I couldn't play. I really wanted to play and found it difficult being there. I stopped going along and then I stopped talking to the team on the text group. They reached out a few times, but I ignored it. I just couldn't respond. Not playing rugby made me feel useless, so I wanted to forget it existed.

Eventually, I got my pre-op appointment. I went to the hospital for some blood tests and had my height and weight taken. I was shocked that over the short time not playing rugby I had gone up to 20 stone. They told me that they would have to talk to the anaesthesiologist. This scared me. I thought they wouldn't do the operation. I made a deal with myself that I would go on a diet and work out every day if they said it was okay to go ahead. Thankfully, they decided I could have the operation.

I turned up to the hospital on the day of the procedure, worried and happy: worried I might not wake up or something would go wrong, and happy that I was finally getting fixed. I remember going into surgery and being injected in the arm. A nurse asked what alcohol I liked to drink. I remember saying I like my whiskies and was about to talk about Guinness when I must have passed out. I woke up in a different location, but I was still thinking about Guinness. Then the pain kicked in almost immediately when I woke up.

It was agony: my leg was on fire. I was given some morphine, and I drifted off into a pleasant slumber. When I woke again, I was in a ward with five other beds. My mouth and throat hurt so badly, I grabbed the jug of water next to my bed. No matter how much I drank, I was still thirsty. A nurse came over and informed me that I would be staying the night and asked if I was hungry. 'I always am,' I said. I was brought a dry ham sandwich, some ready-salted crisps, and an apple that looked older than Mother Teresa. It was too painful to eat anything.

I asked for more water and drank the whole jug. Suddenly, I thought, how will I get to the bathroom? The friendly nurse who brought me my sandwich asked if I would like a fizzy drink. I was brought a diet coke, which I drank with relish. A few minutes later, the toilet problem raised its head. I rang my buzzer and asked if I could go for a wee, to be told no. I was given a cardboard bottle and told to wee into that. Over the next few hours, I must have urinated about 15 times. I was getting embarrassed at having to ring the buzzer every time I wanted a wee. I kept apologising to the nurses and was eventually told off and had to promise the nurse I wouldn't say sorry again. I broke that promise minutes later when I needed another wee and then began to apologise for apologising. Eventually, my bladder dried up, and I took some more painkillers and drifted off to sleep.

When I woke I felt much better and was given a microwaved breakfast. My throat still hurt, so they gave me four yoghurts and took the breakfast away. The consultant came round and informed me that I would begin my torture schedule – I mean rehab – that day. He explained that it was important that we begin right away, and I would have to perform some tasks like walking up and down some stairs before I could go home. 10am rolled round, and so did my torturer. Professionally they are called physiotherapists.

The first task was to get my leg to bend 90 degrees. I was to sit in a wheelchair and place my foot on the footrest. I managed to bend my knee 90 degrees no problem, but my foot wasn't on the footrest platform. Now, this was because of my height. My torturer didn't account for the fact that being a tall person with longer legs, when I sat in the wheelchair my bum would be lower than my knee. She didn't quite get this concept and duly got on her knees, grabbed my ankle, and forced my foot backwards on to the platform. This meant my knee was now bent way over 90 degrees. This caused excruciating pain, forcing me to turn on to my left side and flick my foot off the platform. My torturer looked at me and geared up for another grab.

Just then, one of the nurses who were looking after me came to my rescue and informed the physiotherapist that if I was sitting in that chair, I wouldn't get my foot on the rest. She stood up as if to appraise me like a mechanic looking at a job on a customer's car. She turned to the nurse, laughed, and said, 'Oh yeah, I should get the seat cushion.' She then walked off. I thanked the nurse and told her I was trying to tell her it wouldn't bend that far. Then she laughed at me and patted me on the shoulder.

That wasn't the end of my torture; that day I was taken to a room full of instruments of pain. The physio got me on a treadmill to do some slow hobbling. I was then made to climb a short set of stairs, and next I was made to lie down on a mat and did some bending of the leg. Every second was painful, and I was hoping they would keep me in, and I could get some of that sweet, sweet morphine. Unfortunately, my captor set me free and said I could go home after the doctor saw me.

The doctor came around and said he was happy for me to go – no more morphine for me. I had a prescription for strong painkillers and a weekly group physio appointment. I had six weeks of intensive rehab to do and longer recovery to get back to running if I wanted to. I started rehab quickly, and surprisingly I got mobility back quite fast. However, I still wasn't exercising, and I was eating rubbish all the time.

Just as before the operation, my inability to play rugby due to my knee caused me to hide away from it, stop watching my team-mates, or even talking to the rugby lads. I can't completely put my finger on why I did this. I have a couple of theories. Number one – it was too painful to be around as I really wanted to play. I wanted to be part of it and couldn't. So, out of sight, out of mind. Number two – I was happy to use my knee as an excuse to be lazy, and I was embarrassed to let my rugby mates see how big I had gotten. If I am honest, it was probably a mixture of both.

I was continuing my rehab sessions and even paid to do more. I was having regular appointments with my surgeon. Every time I saw him, I would get on the scales, and my weight would have gone up. He would tell me that the heavier I was, the more chance the microfractures would fail. I would listen and nod. I would tell myself with all the willpower in the world that I would not stuff my face anymore and that I needed to start exercising.

But then I would get home and my willpower would have strangely disappeared. I would grab a family bag of crisps, some cake and some biscuits and wait for Charlotte to come home so we could cook our dinner. I would have double helpings of dinner and a pudding. A few hours later, I would have more cake or crisps now with a few cans of beer.

This was every day. The more I ate, the more I was embarrassed by my weight and what I looked like. The more I hid away, the lonelier I got. The lonelier I was the more comfort I found in food. This was a vicious cycle that I knew I was in and couldn't break. I understood I should do something about it but chose not to. When I chose not to do anything I began to see myself as a bad person.

I started to go back to work – at the time I was working nights. I found myself starting to eat in secret. I would wake up in the afternoon for a night shift and have a snack. Charlotte would get back from work and we would eat dinner. I would take some sandwiches to work and at some point in the night I would have a takeaway. I would also go to the shop and get some biscuits or chocolate to have with my coffees that ended up more sugar than coffee. Then when it was home time, I would text Charlotte to see if she wanted me to pick up a McDonald's breakfast. I would buy what she wanted and order two meals for me and I would eat one on the way home while driving.

This kept going on day after day. I could feel myself getting physically worse; my knee was going backwards because of my weight. All the rehab work would be for nothing if I carried on like this. I couldn't get in my car properly as I would have to put all my body weight on my bad leg to get in. When no one was watching, I would get in my car like an old-fashioned lady, bum first.

I went to my next appointment with my surgeon and when I got off the scales, he looked sad. I asked about the damage, and he said 23 stone. This wasn't good. I felt like rubbish, I was so embarrassed and I actually apologised. He asked me what I thought was a strange question: he asked what I wanted to do with my life. I said I didn't really know. He asked if I would like to exercise. 'Yes,' I said.

'What exercise?' he replied. I didn't know what exercise because I didn't really want into do any, so I said the first thing that came to my head and that was running. He looked surprised and then flatly told me with my knee and my size, I wouldn't be able to run 1km as it would damage my microfractures. He prescribed me a walk of up to 2km every day. I left and never took up his prescription. I thought it was stupid: what was 2km going to do? This cycle went from day to day to year to year. Over these years when we went on holiday, I could hardly fit in a plane seat. I refused to take my top off and would get in the pool or sea with my top on. Despite knowing that I looked a mess and being embarrassed around the pool, it didn't stop me eating plate after plate of the finest all-inclusive buffet and drinking multiple beers for breakfast. I wouldn't get in my best mate's new hot tub using the chlorine excuse. I can't help but think that I missed out on a lot of experiences and happiness in that part of my life. By the time we got to my best friend Simon's wedding, I was 24 stone and in mental and physical pain daily.

And that brings me right back to that fateful night at Simon's house in late 2019, when the switch was turned on in my head. That night I made the decision. No more. No more self-loathing and no more binge eating. But what was I going to do to fix myself?

Chapter 5

Alone

THE DAY after the night before. That fateful night where the switch went on in my head. I knew I would change my life. I can't fully explain how I knew: I just knew I felt different. I knew I never wanted to put myself through what I had been through while watching those wedding videos again.

I didn't say any of this out loud. I didn't tell Charlotte what I was thinking. I didn't tell my friends or co-workers. I kept it to myself and began to plan. I spent most of that day hungover but excited about how I was going to achieve weight loss and become healthy. I researched the internet, literally all day. I read pages and pages of advice and guidance. I wrote ideas down in a little notebook. I wrote ideas about going on the carnivore diet. I then wrote information about going on a vegan diet. I wrote ideas about different weightlifting programmes. I found a guy who transformed his body by doing yoga. It was remarkable

– he had walked with a cane because he was so big and now he was a slim yoga god.

I then came across an article about a book called *Living with a SEAL*. It was a non-fiction book about a rich marketing man who employed an ex-Navy SEAL to live with him and train him. I couldn't believe how the article portrayed this Navy SEAL guy. His mindset seemed crazy and possibly fake. I didn't believe any one person could be so focused on pushing themselves to the physical limit, just because they could. I thought, 'What's the point?' I ordered the book and went on trying to plan what I was going to do.

Over the next few days I started cutting my food intake. I would try to halve my portion sizes and cut out sugar. I found this so difficult. Some days were a success, and I would eat healthily. Then I would kill my progress by eating a whole large pizza and several cakes the following day. I knew this wasn't working and I still had not decided what type of physical exercise I was going to do. I was concerned about my knees and what they could handle. I struggled on with my diet for a few days, determined not to quit.

The book I had ordered arrived on a Friday. That weekend I read that book from cover to cover in two days and enjoyed every word. I wanted to know more about this Navy SEAL and his crazy feats of endurance and strength. In the book, his name was not mentioned at all. After some light research on the net, I found out the guy was called David Goggins. I devoured every bit of information I could about him. I was fascinated by his mindset and how he could run ultra marathons with broken bones and kidney failure.

I started to get the idea that I wanted a mindset like his. I fantasised about being an ultra-hardcore BadArse, and to be able to push my body through pain. I wanted to fix my broken bones with duct tape and do what he did. Researching David Goggins opened the world of ultra running to me. It was a world I didn't know existed. Why would anyone want to run longer distances than a marathon? In fact, why would anyone want to run a marathon? The more I read and the more YouTube videos I watched on ultra running, the more I began to understand that this was the ultimate sense of achievement. I found a great attraction in the idea that fewer than one per cent of the world's population run ultra marathons and many people don't even know they exist.

Inspired by ultra running and David Goggins, I knew I wanted to try running. I also knew it might not be a good idea, being 24 stone and having a weak knee. I wanted to check out advice on running at my weight and with my knee problem. Everything I found said don't do it, lose weight first and then try. I found one article that said that running was actually good for the knee. I decided to listen to that one article and ignore everything else.

Again, I didn't tell anyone what I was up to as I thought they would stop me. I brought a pair of running shoes and some new cycling shorts to wear under my normal shorts as I didn't want to get the dreaded chub rub on my thighs that I had read about. Once I had the gear, I planned to go out and just try to run a short distance. However, I couldn't bring myself to do it. I couldn't go out and run. What if someone saw me? What would they think? I talked myself out of going for a run because I thought people would think that this fat boy has no business running. I imagined people leaning out of car windows shouting abuse at me. I imagined groups of youths following me and throwing things at me. I was so embarrassed and scared to be seen, so I tried to forget the idea and continue with my cycle of success and failure dieting. For a couple of days, I tried to forget running, but the videos kept popping up on YouTube. I was firmly in the David Goggins and ultra running algorithm.

The pull of trying to run became too much – I couldn't get it out of my head. I waited until dark so no one would see me; I put my new gear on and went out to run. Where I live, there are some beautiful country lanes and walkways with no streetlights. So that's where I headed. I had to allow my eyes to adapt to the pitch black first and I tried to run. Within seconds, I was out of breath with sweat pouring from me like a sprinkler. I stopped running and walked for a bit and then ran for ten seconds. I did this run-walk method until my phone said I had completed 1km and then I walked home. 1km doesn't sound much, but for a 24-stone bloke with a bad knee, it was enough.

I jumped in the bath, feeling pretty proud of myself. I had no pain in my knee at all, which was positive. I did the same every other day for a couple of weeks. I would wait for it to get dark and make my way to where there were no streetlights or people. I did the run-walk thing for 1km every time. I really started to enjoy this time alone in the dark. It was a great stress relief after a day at work. I would get home after my pitch black 1km and feel great. I understand how crazy it sounds to be so embarrassed about your size and what people would think of you if they saw you running – so embarrassed that you only run in the dark – but it made sense in my mind.

I can tell you that I scared a few people on my nightly excursions. Not only would I run in the dark, I would also only run in black clothing with no lights or reflection strips. I remember one poor lady who was walking her dog. I gave her the fright of her life when she saw this 6ft 4in, 24-stone shadow shuffling toward her out of the dark, panting heavily. She made an audible gasp and took a step into a muddy ditch. What made things worse, when I stopped and tried to apologise and explain what I was doing, I could see she was terrified. The only thing I could do was to turn around and slowly shuffle off before she started to scream.

I kept doing this for a few months. I was covering further distances with my nightly run-walk – I was up to 3km a night and I was back under 24 stone. This spurred me on to keep running.

I kept up the research, watching hundreds of running-related videos online. I took inspiration from these videos, mainly the ones where people had transformed their bodies through exercise. Seeing that they had been able to turn their lives around gave me the push to keep going with mine. By luck I was in a second-hand book shop and found a book called *In Search of Al Howie*, about a troubled ultra-runner who pulled off some fantastic feats of endurance. This guy wouldn't just run and win ultra marathons; he would run to the race and then run home. Once I finished that book, I needed to set my own running goal. I toyed with the idea of a 10km or a half marathon. This didn't feel enough. While on my nightly run, I thought: 'Why not pick an ultra marathon as my main goal and work backwards from there?' I could try and achieve progressively greater distances – 5km, 10km, half marathon, marathon and then an ultra.

After my bath, which had become a ritual after a run, I made sure I wrote down my goal and some milestones. Some days I didn't want to run and there were days where I was tempted to binge on cake. I would look in my notebook to give me inspiration, especially on days where my willpower was lacking. My running was going well, but I still didn't have control over my food cravings, although they were getting better. Just doing this run-walk and cutting back on food I had lost over a stone in weight.

I received a letter from the hospital for a check-up appointment with my surgeon. I had the standard test height and weight, and he was pleasantly surprised that I was lighter than the last time I had seen him. We talked about what I had been doing, and he was shocked that my knee was holding up under my weight while running. He told me that 5km of slow running would be the most I could do – anything else could be too much and cause damage. I asked him if he thought I could ever run further, and he said that the way my knee was, I was not likely to get over 10km and to do that, I would have to lose an enormous amount of weight. I decided not to tell him about my ultra marathon dreams, and I ignored his advice. Instead, I listened to my inner Goggins and convinced myself that I would eventually achieve that distance.

In my little notebook, my next goal was 5km non-stop. I concentrated on achieving this goal while eating better. The better I ran, the more control I had over my cravings and I made better food choices. I stopped looking at my weight as often as I used to; sometimes it was disheartening to see how slowly I was losing weight. I focused only on the 5km distance. The closer I got to that goal, the more confidence I had. It was now summertime, and I was still running at night, but it wasn't dark. I seemed to have stopped caring what people might think of me. It was a gradual thing that happened over the early months of 2020, and I didn't realise I was no longer running in the dark until Charlotte mentioned that I could get sunburn running in the heat.

Then one night in late summer, I smashed my 5km goal. I managed to run non-stop for a whole 5km. I was so happy I had done it – milestone achieved! I started to look for 5km races and fun runs to take part in. I now wanted to test myself against other people. I found a Halloween 5km run that was a few months away. This allowed me to continue to train, and I liked the fact it would be done in the dark and in a country lane environment. I thought this race was right up my alley. By the time the race came around, I was 21 stone.

My knee was holding up, and I was regularly running 5km non-stop.

The day of the race came. I was extremely nervous. I kept worrying that I would come last, and people would laugh at me. I felt if I came last all the training and progress would be for nothing, and I was lying to myself for even thinking I could do this. I really had to push myself to get to the event. This was the first time I would be running with people, and I didn't like it.

I tentatively got out of my car with a heavy feeling in my stomach. As I walked up to the registration table I could see people dressed in all sorts of costumes: ghosts, zombies, vampires, and there were even two people dressed as a dragon. There were people of every age and size, and they all seemed to be having fun. The registration staff were really friendly and put me at ease. I didn't know why I was worried – I thought that everyone would be ultra-professional and be treating this like a race.

It was time to go to the start line. I didn't want to be anywhere near the front, so I hung back closer to the middle. Some guy dressed as Frankenstein's monster started to chat to me. He was the first person I told my story to. I told him what I was doing and why I was there. He was very supportive and wished me luck. The hooter went and we all set off. People were screaming and cheering. It was a wonderful atmosphere, and I didn't feel judged at all. I remember thinking 'I wish I could do this every week.'

The runners quickly spread out across the field. Some were dressed to the nines in Halloween gear and others were covered in flashing lights so they could be seen in the dark. There was a turn-around point in a wooded area 2.5km from the start line. The speedy runners got there quickly. When they came back towards us slower runners, they all shouted words of support. I felt great. When we slower runners got to the woods, the organisers had set up some surprises. There were people dressed in costumes jumping from behind trees, scaring people, there were people shooting water guns at us. It was great fun. I hit the turn-around point and started my journey back to where we began. To my surprise, there were still what looked like hundreds of runners going towards the turn-around point. I wasn't going to be last, unless something went drastically wrong. I saw the lights of the finish line and heard the speakers blaring out Halloween tunes, and I picked up my pace.

I wanted to finish strong. My heart was pumping, and my lungs were screaming for more oxygen as I approached the line. I thought I might have stepped up the pace too much. I couldn't stop or slow down now: I had to hold on and cross the line. And I did it; I held on and crossed that line. While I was doubled over gasping for air, a big shiny medal was placed around my neck.

I had never been happier. That medal seems like the embodiment of all the training I had done. It was the reward after the hard work and it's my favourite medal to this day. I walked towards the water station, and waiting for me was Frankenstein's monster. He gave me a hug and said he waited to see how I got on. I was so touched by this act of kindness that I nearly broke down in tears. I wish I knew his name because I would like to thank him. That one act of kindness had a profound effect on me. He made me realise that most runners belong to a supportive community, and it doesn't matter what size you are or what your ability is – if you run, you are a runner. Thank you, Frankenstein's monster.

The next goal was 10km. I trained with the aim of hitting the distance after Christmas or into the New Year. I stepped up my distance in training, I didn't really have a training plan, and I just ran for a little bit longer every week. While I did this, I also looked for other 5km races to enter. I wanted to experience the camaraderie and support of the fun run/race scene that I experienced on Halloween. I entered a 5km night race along the Meon Valley.

I had to buy a head torch for it, as it was mandatory to wear one. I made the rookie mistake of not testing it before I got to the race. When I arrived, the organisers checked my entry email and turned my head torch on and off. Great, it worked; I had passed the first test. What I had neglected to do was try the torch on my head. I was on the starting line when I realized that I had forgotten this important step. I began to panic because for the life of me I could not get it on my bloody head. The straps seemed to be the wrong way around and too small.

The rules said you had to have a head torch on at all times. The seconds ticked by and still I was failing to get it on. It also didn't help that it was pitch black and every time someone looked at me their head torch blinded me momentarily. The start gun went off and I had to hold the torch to my head for the whole race. I am glad I couldn't see anyone's face in the dark because I am sure they would be looking at me funny. They probably thought: 'Why doesn't that muppet just wear his head torch?'

At the end of the race my arm was aching. I got my medal, some hot food and a free beer. As I sat in my car, I saw that the straps had flipped inside out, and it should have been an easy fix. I put the issue down to pre-race anxiety.

I then entered a 5km Santa race at Christmas. I was looking forward to this one. Everyone who entered got a Santa suit and the route was along the seafront. When I got to the race area the atmosphere was brilliant. There was a group of drummers dressed as Santas knocking out some tribal beats, which really pumped me up. I got chatting to a lady at the start line and she told me that after this 5km she would continue to run home to Chichester, so she would end up running around 50km. I thought she was amazing for doing it, and told her so.

The start buzzer sounded and off we plodded. I found myself overtaking a few people, which surprised me. This wasn't technically a race; it was a fun run for Christmas, for goodness sake. However, in my head this suddenly became a race. Everyone I overtook gave me a boost and pushed me to the finish line. I also got overtaken by loads of people, but they didn't count. I collected my medal and my free warm mince pie and enjoyed it while looking out to sea. With a proud smile I reflected on the year and the progress I had made. I was extremely proud and happy with myself, and I was feeling great. I was now down to 20 stone, and life was getting better.

My running was slow during this time. As you can imagine, trying to shift all that weight on a bad knee wasn't going to be quick. I didn't really pay attention to my times during this stage of my running. It was all about distance and being able to achieve it without stopping.

After basking in my achievements as the sea lapped the shore, I went home for my ritual bath and planned to have a week off running over the Christmas holidays. I was still struggling with food and decided to let myself go and have some chocolates and other Christmas treats. This was a mistake. I wasn't ready to casually eat treats and stop like a normal person. I found it easy to slip back into the same eating patterns as that 24-stone guy. My week off extended to two weeks and I lied to myself after New Year's that I would get back at it. I would enjoy the festive celebrations and then back to work. I knew what I was doing but did it anyway. I became angry at myself, slipping back into that self-hatred.

After welcoming the New Year in, I had to have a couple of days to get over my hangover. Then I weighed myself; I had shockingly put nearly half a stone back on. NO WAY! This couldn't be right. But sadly it was. With the mood this put me in I nearly packed in the running there and then. I took myself off and sulked in a corner for a while. I had a firm word with myself. I thought of the promise I had made to myself. I looked in my notebook of goals. This gave me the little nudge I needed to start training again. I began pushing towards my 10km goal. My little slip over Christmas was what I needed. It showed me how easily I could fall back into my old ways and how much I didn't want that to happen.

I took everything a lot more seriously from that point on. I kept working with no real plan, so I began to buy technical running books that talked about training plans. I found all the talk of sessions, intervals and hill reps confusing. They all seemed the same to me and I gave them all a swift ignoring. I just kept my focus on running further every week. I can't remember at what point it was, but I hit the 8km mark. This was a big thing for me, and I celebrated and cherished the fact I hit my lucky number eight. I knew that if I could run 8km, I could definitely run 10km even if I had to crawl on my hands and knees. It was a rest day, but I had itchy feet. I wanted to get out and try 10km, but I behaved myself and rested.

The very next day I did it, 10km in the bag. I loved how easy things started to feel. Running is so much easier when you're under 20 stone.

I entered a 10km race that took place on a sandy beach. I thought it looked fun. It was 5km out and 5km back. But there was a problem: you weren't racing just people, you were racing the tide. The slower you were, the higher up the beach the tide pushed you. The higher you got, the dryer and softer the sand was, making it more energy-sapping to your legs.

I made two big mistakes that day. Number one, I went out way too hard and by the time I got to the 5km turning point, I was absolutely knackered. I had let the fun, chatty atmosphere make me giddy and I used up all my energy. Number two, I used new gear on race day. When I ran, I would use cycling shorts to help stop my thighs rubbing together and starting a fire. I had got to the turning point, and I had slowed right down. The tide had pushed me up the beach with a few other slower-paced people.

I now had a choice: run on the soft, dry sand and kill my legs, or allow my feet to get wet from the water while running on the compacted sand. I picked the water and that was a bad idea. There were wooden wave-breakers every now and then, meaning I had to jump over them into progressively deeper water. This caused my new under-shorts to get wet with salty water. They began to droop around my crotch, and I was suffering the worst chub rub you could ever imagine. The insides of my thighs were on fire: every ten steps a layer of skin would be rubbed off. I then moved up to the soft, dry sand to get away from the water. This made everything worse, and my feet started to suffer with sand getting in my shoes. The dry sand sapped all the energy out of my legs, and it felt like I was dragging two heavy bags of sand along.

I had to walk the last 3km, dragging two dead legs and walking like a cowboy so the inside of my thighs wouldn't touch. I collected my medal, which I felt I didn't deserve, and quickly left. My ritual bath after a run was a hellscape of burning, skinless thighs and badly blistered toes. I spent the next few days liberally applying Sudocrem at every possible moment. I did learn that pacing and race strategy was important and not to wear new gear on race day.

I was now regularly running 10km non-stop. I started to dabble with something I learned called negative splits. I was trying to run the second half of a 10km faster than the first. I entered another 10km race, which was a little further afield in the South Downs National Park. I had a pacing plan ready with the goal of a negative split. Everything was going great until I hit the hills of the South Downs. The first hill came, and it was slow and long but not too steep. I saw people walking it and thought: 'This isn't so bad.' I went down the other side and thought, 'This is easy street,' until I made my way along a leafy path behind a pub, where I met the monster I needed to scale.

For a moment, I thought about stopping and having a few pints before tackling it. It wasn't long, but it was steep. It was in direct sunlight with no shade. The top of the hill was shaded by a wooded area. I heard someone say there was a drinks station at the top, so I put my head down and ran. I kept going, although as I closed in on the top of the monster, my speed had slowed, and my breathing had turned to gasps. I crested the hill and stumbled into the cool, shaded wood to find no drinks station. More alarmingly I had crested a false summit, and the hill continued up through the trees.

Oh well, head down I attempted to scale the rest of the monster. Thankfully, there was a drinks station at the real summit. I grabbed a bottle of water and kept running. The route took me back down the other side of the hill and along a closed-off country road. I realised I was now on another hill looking down. From my vantage point I could see the finish line. I decided to give it everything I had left in the tank. I attacked the last 1.5km as hard as I could and crossed the line. I was happy because I didn't have to stop. This medal I felt I deserved, and I wore it with pride. I didn't hit the negative splits, but it led me to think back to the running sessions that I had swiftly ignored. I wondered if they would help me to hit a negative split.

I was now 19 stone. I had lost five stone from running and trying to eating right. I could run 10km easy, well easy-ish as long as there was no salt water to set my thighs on fire. I felt and looked better. The feeling when people commented on how much weight I had lost was pure happiness. I had to buy new clothes as mine had become too big. I found I could get out of the car easily with no pain or grunting. The most noticeable thing was the improvement in my mental health: I was happy.

I started to push my distance further and further. I began to run after work with my mate Dave. We would only do 5km, but we would do it faster and faster every time we tried. One Friday Dave asked me what my plan for the weekend was. I said I was running 15km non-stop. He wished me luck with a smirk. I am not sure if he believed me. I went home for the weekend and prepped all my stuff for the longest distance I had ever attempted.

I woke early on Saturday morning, got my gear on and off I went. I took some water and energy gels for nutrients. The first 10km was fine, no issues; I had picked a flat route, and I had got past the 11km mark when my stomach started to bubble. I had heard of people suffering from the runner's squits. Luckily, I had never had the misfortune of experiencing it. I looked on maps to find the nearest toilet and it was in a supermarket a few hundred metres off my route.

I had no choice. I had to get there and fast. Clutching my bum cheeks, I waddled my way into the gents. Horror hit me when I saw that the toilets were disgustingly filthy. There was urine and excrement everywhere. Someone or a group of people had had a poo party in there. I realised it would have been much more pleasant if I had gone in nature behind a tree and used leaves to clean up. Anyway, I was here now and had to make it work. I spent several minutes making sure I wouldn't get anyone's business on me and then did my thing and left quickly, hoping I hadn't caught anything. I made a mental note to take toilet paper on a long run in case I got caught short again.

I felt much better over the remainder of the run; my legs ached and my lower back started to hurt but I was relatively okay. When I eventually got home, I had run 16km. I was over the moon; my knee was fine, and I was happy. My first thought was that I had proven my surgeon wrong. He had said I would struggle to run 10km and I had just smashed it. That night, I treated myself to a few glasses of red wine.

When I woke up on the Sunday morning, OH MY GOD! I felt like ten buses had hit me. My head was pounding as the wine had dehydrated me. I couldn't move my legs. They were stiff but when I stood, they were like jelly. I realised that my mind was willing to run far, but my body wasn't fully ready.

I was still feeling bad on the Monday going into work. I could barely make it up the steps to our office, and when Dave saw me, he laughed. He asked me how it went, and I told him every gritty detail. He was happy for me, and we discussed that maybe it was time to follow a training plan. I told him I would but while I searched for training plans, he made a phone call without me knowing.

Chapter 6
Help

I WAS up and off to work as usual. By now I had secured a job working for Babcock International, initially stationed at HMS *Sultan* in Gosport as head of support services for a defence training contract. I was lucky enough to get on to one of their high-potential programmes and they paid for my degree in business management. Babcock were a great company to work for and as I completed my degree, I got the opportunity to experience working in one of their bids teams in army HQ, Andover. Here I worked on a number of winning bids in the defence industry. I eventually returned to HMS *Sultan* as contract director. I worked with lots of wonderful people and made a few firm friends.

As I walked in that day, Dave passed me a phone number. He said he had talked to his mate, who was a running coach and triathlete. He told me that he had chatted to him about me. Dave went on to say that his mate would be happy to help me and give me some

HELP

guidance on my running. This made me nervous; I imagined an American type of drill instructor shouting at me to 'move my fat ass'. I didn't know what to expect. I had got this far on my own: did I really need a coach? I put the thought of a coach to the back of my mind but kept the number.

Then one day Matt, the health and safety guy, made a visit to the office that Dave and I shared. Matt began to talk to Dave about a mutual friend they had who was an ultra-runner. This ultra-runner was currently trying for the female record on the Land's End to John O'Groats route. They were tracking her on Matt's phone and watching some YouTube videos of the run. I thought what she was doing was so cool. I wanted to do it, and it made me wonder, could I? In my mind it was possible, but I would definitely need some help for a challenge so big.

As I was thinking this, the conversation between Matt and Dave changed from the ultra-runner to the coach. They began to talk about a man called Coach Dave. Coach Dave was the trainer for a woman who was running Land's End to John O'Groats. I was listening intently to their conversation. It suddenly dawned on me that Coach Dave was the same coach that was offering me support.

Once Matt left the office, I brought the subject up with Work Dave again. He went through and explained some of the stuff Coach Dave had done. He mentioned that he had done triathlons, coached pro ultra-runners, and coached the British army in Nordic skiing, among other things. I thought, 'What would this guy train me for when he's dealing with loads of pros?' I was reluctant, but Work Dave talked me into sending Coach Dave a text to see what the deal was. After all, if I didn't like it, I didn't have to go through with anything.

I texted the number and within the next 30 minutes I was talking on the phone to Coach Dave. He asked a whole load of questions including what my motivations were, what it was that I wanted to achieve and why. At first, I found it difficult to talk openly – I was nervous. He managed to put me at ease, and I told him everything. I told him that I was 24 stone and had worked hard to get to 19 stone. I told him about how I hated myself and felt shame when I was that big. I explained how I couldn't even look at myself in pictures or the mirror. We discussed how I found inspiration in people like David Goggins and other ultra-runners.

The conversation moved to what I had done so far, and I told him about running myself into the ground trying to achieve longer distances. He listened to what I said and showed no judgement. I found myself moving from nervousness to hope. Coach Dave told me that some structure in my training would get me where I wanted to be. A wide smile broke across my face when he said he would be happy to coach me. Inside I was a mixture of excitement and nervousness. I was nervous that I wouldn't be able to do what he asked of me. I didn't want him to think I was pants compared to the other people he coached. I was excited about what this might mean for my future. Where could I go with this support?

He gave me instructions on the run he wanted me to complete that night. Once completed, he wanted me to send him the Garmin data to review. I guessed this was some sort of baseline test. I agreed to do what he asked. I ended the call, and I didn't know what I had been worried about. Coach Dave was such a nice bloke. I couldn't help but think if he was going to help me when he was helping people at a much higher standard than me, I would give 110 per cent in everything he asked me to do. I excitedly told Work Dave about everything Coach Dave and I had talked about. I thanked Work Dave for putting me in touch with a coach. For the rest of the working day, I fantasised about running Land's End to John O'Groats.

That night after work, I set about completing the run Coach Dave asked me to do. The run was a straightforward 10km. I went out wanting to impress him. For this reason, I ran hard from the start. I attacked that 10km right from the first step. All my previous learning around pacing went out of the window. It felt like I was flying, with the wind behind me, giving me a slight boost. I was clever and picked a flat route from my house with few to no hills to slow me down.

Predictably, I started to run out of energy during the later stages of the run. In the last 3km I slowed right down to almost a walk. At the end my lungs were burning, and the cool air stung my insides as I gasped in and out. I was happy the run was good; I felt light and quick until the end. I texted Coach Dave the stats from my Garmin watch. I sat there eagerly waiting for a reply. I was thinking there was still time for him to drop me as a coachee. My phone started to ring, and it was him.

The first thing he said was: 'You went out too fast.' He knew exactly what I was doing, and he told me I needed to slow down and find an even pace and finish without getting knackered. On my next run, he wanted me to slow right down and run an even pace. I couldn't get my head around it; every run I wanted to go out hard. To me that was the only way to progress. When I did what he asked, I didn't even feel I had run at all.

I now know he was trying to get a good baseline on what I found to be an easy pace. I had to get it into my head that ultra marathons were not just about sprinting: sometimes you would have to walk. I would need to find a pace that was comfortable over long distances, and then we would work to increase the distance and speed. Over the years Dave coached me, it became a common theme and joke that I would go out fast and waste all my energy before the finish. My wife probably thinks the same.

Coach Dave asked me to spend a couple of days doing what I was doing while he put a programme together for me. I gave him my Garmin account details, and he created a whole programme in my account for me. Pretty soon I was doing all the sessions I had been actively ignoring. I was now doing proper session intervals, tempo runs, hill runs, and weekly slow long runs.

I was loving it. The structure allowed me to be more disciplined and I started to get obsessed with shaving seconds off my times. I felt like a new person. To everyone, including my long-suffering wife, I had probably become a running bore. I would talk about nothing else other than my most recent training session and my fancy new running shoes.

After I completed my sessions, Coach Dave would review the stats and ask me questions on how I felt physically during and after. He introduced me to the Rate of Perceived Exertion scale that allowed me to put a number on how I felt during a run. I would then be given advice on what to do differently to get better. I really enjoyed the structure of the training and I loved chatting to him about what I needed to do next. Quickly I started to feel I was getting stronger and faster. I could go longer distances without getting knackered, and all the data confirmed my feelings. I felt like a real runner now.

Some people will call me a masochist, and they often do. Hill reps quickly became my favourite session. I found the perfect hill close by. This hill was exactly half a km up. I would run the 2.5km to the hill and run up and down it between five and ten times, and then I would run back home. Yes, it was exhausting, it killed my quads and burned my lungs, but it made me feel strong. It turned my legs into slabs of pure muscle. I enjoyed hill reps more than any other session. My next favourite session was intervals, but they weren't a patch on my beloved hills. I liked them because I was seeing the best results from them. Everything was going well.

At the time, I was still looking for a diet I could stick to that would complement my running. This wasn't an easy task until I found a thing called intermittent fasting. It sounded right up my street. There was no messing about with portion sizes or things like macros. For me it was the lazy way to diet: all you had to do was not eat. I started the process of fasting for 16 hours a day and having an eight-hour eating window. Gradually, this 16-hour fast went up to a 20-hour fast with only a four-hour eating window daily.

For me, intermittent fasting was great. With all the training I was doing, I could basically eat what I wanted in my eating window. I could eat burgers, chips and pizza and it was nearly impossible to overeat in terms of calories. I noticed the benefits to my training very quickly. When I ran, I felt lighter. I started to lose weight quickly, but it made me feel stronger. I would recover faster from heavy training sessions and my long runs.

My fasting became an obsession for me. It allowed me to be totally in control of eating for once. I would keep to my fasting regime religiously. Charlotte, the kids and I would go camping in Dorset with Simon and Rob's families. They would all be eating and cooking together, and I would just sit there and watch. Everyone eating in front of me never bothered me once, although it didn't stop them trying to tempt me. I would only drink water and black coffee and nothing else until my eating window. Later this became a struggle as I stepped up my training. I would have to eat on my long runs to give me energy. This felt like I was losing that control I now had over the way I ate. On the days of my long runs, I had to lengthen my eating window from four hours to eight. I made sure

I fasted for at least 16 hours. It was all psychological. I was terrified of ballooning back up to 24 stone.

Fasting and my new structured training had got me down to 16 stone, a loss of eight stone. That's the size of a small child. I felt and looked great. My mental health was in the best place it had ever been. Outside of running, my relationship with my wife and kids was much better because I was happy with myself. It's true when they say that, to love others, you have to love yourself first. I was pushing myself professionally. I got several promotions at work and started to get noticed by my managers as a reliable member of the team. I truly felt that everything was great, and I knew it was inevitable I would achieve an ultra marathon. It would only be a matter of time.

That time, though, was extended due to the third nationwide COVID lockdown, which began on 5 January 2021. All races were cancelled, but that allowed me to concentrate on training even more. I don't think many people would say this, but the COVID lockdown was kind to me. It was a difficult time for many people across the world. Many people sadly lost their lives. Families were kept separated when they needed each other the most, and many people's livelihoods suffered.

For me it gave me time to focus on running – there was nothing else to do but concentrate on exercise and weight loss. I became so much faster, and I could hold that pace for longer and longer distances. The intervals and hills were paying off. When outdoor activities were finally allowed again on 12 April, I decided to put my newfound speed to the test. I entered a local 5km race. For many people, this was their first event once everything opened up again. As a result, there was a party atmosphere. I felt a real community spirit. People were happy to be back around people again doing what they loved.

This atmosphere didn't stop me from having the old imposter syndrome, even though I was now much slimmer, and I had all the fancy new running gear: I was no longer running in baggy rugby shirts or old hoodies; I had proper running tops, proper shorts, and those cool wrap-around sunglasses. Even so, I still had the old image of myself in my mind, and I think I always will. No matter the gear, no matter the slimness, or how good I get at running, that 24-stone bloke is still lurking in the shadows of my mind.

We made our way to the start line. Trying to ignore my negative thoughts, I threw caution to the wind and boldly walked up to where the real slim-looking runners were in their club vests. With the imposter syndrome sitting heavy in my stomach, the starting whistle went. IT WAS ON! Time to put the training to the test.

I went out hard within the first couple of minutes. I wanted to get away from the bulk of people and have an open run. The race consisted of two loops around a lake. The course was flat but there were some wet and muddy parts from heavy rain a few days previously. I didn't want to get bogged down in these areas. My plan was to stick with the fast runners for as long as possible. To my complete surprise, I was hanging in there.

I knew this was going to be a quick 5km. I was going that fast, I even caught up to the back of the pack on my second loop of the lake. I crossed the finish line just outside the top 20; my time was 22 minutes 41 seconds. It was my quickest 5km ever. What a feeling: goodbye imposter syndrome and hello confidence. The annoying thing was that my watch had recorded it as just under 5km and didn't register it as a new 5km personal best. Talking to another finisher as I tried to get my lungs to breathe normally again, I told him of my disappointment that my watch was off by 0.2km for my personal best. He had exactly the same watch, and he was over the 5km. Maybe I had a more efficient race line.

I now immersed myself in the running community. I bought and read all the running books I could get hold of, *The Art of Running*, *Dead Man Running*: all the classics. Once I couldn't find any more running books,

I read books about triathlons and other endurance challenges. I listened exclusively to running podcasts and watched only ultra marathon videos on YouTube, which became a daily obsession. These things gave me inspiration to keep going, and I started to push harder. I wanted to be like these people in the book and do what they were doing.

Coach Dave continued to tell me to slow down and have a rest now and then, but I stopped taking rest days and would hit the gym when I should have been relaxing and allowing my body to recover. By now, I was running half-marathon distances on my weekly long runs. I should have listened to Coach Dave and slowed down because I got my first injury from running. I was doing one of my favourite hill rep sessions, and I felt a tight pull deep in my right bum cheek.

It wasn't too painful to start with. It was more of a tight aching. I ran through it and continued to train for the next few days. Then one morning, the aching was so bad it caused me to limp while I walked. I tried to foam roll the pain away, but it wouldn't touch the painful area. I tried to use a massage gun, but that couldn't get anywhere near it. It looked weird, a grown man pushing a massage gun into his bum cheek. I even slapped a TENS machine – an electrical nerve stimulator – on my arse and tried to electrocute the pain away.

Coach Dave advised me to go and see a physio. I decided to pay to see one, so I didn't have to wait for the NHS. They told me that I had aggravated my piriformis, a key muscle in the gluteal region that plays a crucial role in hip movement and stability. I left with some stretches for it that would loosen it up and some exercises to strengthen my glutes. This time I had no choice but to listen to the advice; I rested and did the stretching. Within two weeks, I was back running and slowly upped my distance back to half marathons again. I now knew that rest was important. No rest can cause pain.

To test my piriformis, I entered a trail run in the South Downs in May 2021. I chose the half marathon distance and knew it would be difficult due to the many hills. I wanted to put strain on my injury to see what happened. I promised Coach Dave that if I had the slightest pain, I would pull out. I made my way to a small church hall at the bottom of a massive hill. As I was walking down the hill, I was hoping that I wouldn't have to run back up it as it would have been a killer to start a race. Thankfully, I spied the direction arrows on the course, and they were not pointing at the hill. As I approached the church hall, I could see the start line in a field, but there was no one around at all. I went into the hall, and I was greeted by a friendly older lady. She said I was early, and the other runners don't normally leave the pub until 10 minutes before the start. I thought this was strange; why are all the other runners at the pub? I began to wonder what I had signed up for.

I took a seat and waited. After 15 minutes, people started to show up. There must have been only 40 people who I would be running alongside. This really worried me, as over this distance and terrain, I wasn't quick, and I couldn't hide and blend into the middle of the pack. I felt really out of place. These men and women looked like serious runners. All of them were in club vests, and I was in an England rugby shirt with a colourful running cap and sunglasses. I got the vibe that this was a local race for local people, and I didn't feel welcome.

I contemplated walking away and hiding in the very pub they had all come from. However, I am tight with money, and I had already paid for the race, so I had no choice but to get on with it. Also, I wanted to go home with a medal. There was no start gun, buzzer, or hooter; the official start was the old friendly woman saying, 'Go,' and we went. I instantly thought 'These guys are quick,' and I found myself in last place. The course wasn't marked that well, and I wanted to keep up with some people, so I didn't get lost.

After a while, I stopped trying to keep up and let them all go. I was in last place and remained there all the way around. There were some mean hills to contend with, and I got lost twice. The good news? I didn't have a pain in my behind. I reached the halfway point where the water station was, and the man on duty there was packing away. He said he thought everyone had passed through. I thought, 'Charming mate, we aren't all whippet club runners.' He opened a small bottle of water, poured some into a paper cup and handed it over. It was barely a sip. I asked for more, and he looked inconvenienced by the fact he had to unscrew the lid again, and he filled my cup. It was nowhere near enough water, but I couldn't be bothered to go through the whole thing again and just thanked him and went on my way, wondering why he couldn't give me the bottle.

Thankfully, I saw the finish line in the distance, and yet again it was empty. The only people in sight were the old lady that had greeted me, and the water man that was now sat next to her. I crossed the line, and the old lady congratulated me. She presented me with a small medal, which I immediately placed around my neck. I asked if I was dead last, and she confirmed that I was the last on the course but not officially last because three people had pulled out of the race halfway in. I was over the moon at this and was glad that I got on with it. For me, it was the strangest race and atmosphere I have ever experienced

HELP

at any event. I don't know if I had stumbled on some sort of private race, and I was an outsider that crashed their running party, or whether these guys were all ultra-professional. I wouldn't be quick to go back to that race anytime soon. Next time, I would probably find myself inside a burning Wicker Man.

Chapter 7
Road to Ultra

SO, THE time had now come to book my first ultra marathon. Coach Dave thought I was ready, and I had worked hard so I *knew* I was ready. All I needed to do was pick one and then aim for it. Coach Dave recommended that I book one that was five to six months away. This would give us time to hit the marathon distance in training.

I was like an excited kid in a sweet shop. I didn't know which to pick. There were so many to choose from, all of them providing their own unique challenges.

I thought about going to Loch Ness in Scotland, but the logistics seemed to be a nightmare. It would become very expensive with hotels and trains. I checked out a race that went around the Isle of Wight. I don't know how, but it came out even more expensive than the Loch Ness one even though it was just a ferry ride across the Solent for me.

I started to get internet fatigue. It was past my bedtime and my eyes had become crossed. Just before I gave up and went to bed, I found a unicorn in the form of my perfect race. The race was called Run to the Sea Brighton by a company called Ultraviolet. It was a 50km race in June, starting inland, then running across the South Downs National Park with the big finish on Brighton seafront. This was the one! Best of all it was close enough that Charlotte could drop me at the start and pick me up from Brighton much, much later.

Ignoring the time, I got on the phone and showed Coach Dave the details. He agreed it was perfect, and I should book it ASAP. He also said he would look at some routes close to me that would simulate the terrain to help me prepare. As soon as I put the phone down, I booked it. I couldn't give the organisers my money quickly enough. I started following the organisers' social media accounts so I could stay up to date on race information. I followed the accounts of people who had run the race in the past and looked at their comments. I didn't want to leave any stone unturned, and I absorbed everything I could about Run to the Sea Brighton.

I studied the route until I knew every turn and fork in the roads. I knew it would be difficult due to the elevation; it would be the most I had ever encountered in a race. From experience I knew some of the hills on the South Downs were monsters. I had done a few races on the South Downs before, but they were baby hills compared to what I had signed up for.

I enjoyed researching and buying all new gear for this event. I got myself a new pair of fancy trail trainers. I always ran in the same brand and model of trainer, so I treated myself and I brought two pairs in case of an emergency. When questioned by Charlotte why I had had two pairs of the same trainers delivered, I managed to convince her it was standard practice and part of the mandatory equipment list. I also splurged on a nice new ultra running water vest and bladder, which was a necessity. I would need to carry my own food and water between the aid stations. I also had to carry the mandatory list of emergency items.

I also treated myself to a new running t-shirt and shorts. Now I was a lot slimmer, I was able to buy and fit into all the clothes that were made for runners. I still wasn't ready to run in a vest just yet. I knew I had to break all this gear in before the actual event. It's never a good idea to do an event with gear that you haven't tried and tested. I had learned that the hard way.

Before I found my perfect running trainers, I used to switch between brands and models. One day I was in a sports shop and found a pair of trainers in size 12 with 70 per cent off. They were a bargain, so needless to say I bought them. My current shoes still had plenty of mileage left, so I stuck the new ones in the cupboard. When a local events company did a St Patrick's Day 10km, I thought, 'Great, I will use my new trainers in the cupboard.' It was a very bad idea. The bloody things didn't fit right and tore the skin of my heels. I started the race with white socks and finished with blood-red ones. My heels were sore for weeks after, and I couldn't take the shoes back because I had had them too long. Lesson learned – no new gear on race day.

Coach Dave had done some good research and found somewhere close that simulated the route I would be taking during the ultra. It was a brutal, hilly 16-mile run from Cocking to Queen Elizabeth Country Park in the South Downs. For the next six months, I would run this route often. It immediately started with a long, lung-busting hill from a car park all the way up to some woods at the top. That was just for starters. There were some really steep hills that there was no way you could run up on this route. Sometimes I felt I was almost climbing, as opposed to running. Many times I would have to use my hands while scrambling up a slope. This very quickly became my favourite route to run. I was attracted to it as it was so difficult and made me feel like I had achieved something. The views from some of the hills were spectacular, and on a clear day I could see all the way back to Portsmouth.

The masochist in me started to come out more and I really started to like running when the weather was bad. I loved the feeling of running in the wind and the rain. I especially liked running on the seafront while a storm was rolling in. The grey clouds and crashing waves made the run more exciting. I would get off on the fact I was the only one out in ridiculous weather and I would mock others for staying warm in their homes or in a nice country pub. I think I started to take on the David Goggins mindset a little too much. I continued to read about him and search for inspiration from any source I could.

I began to absorb technical book after technical book on running, diet and fitness. I had read all the books about people who were as big as me changing their lives through sport, discipline and challenge, so the technical books were my next stop. I picked out as many tips and tricks as I could, even silly things like running with your hand like you are holding a butterfly that you don't want to squash. Apparently, doing this keeps you relaxed and takes away any tension in your arms. Another benefit of wanting to know everything about running was that it greatly improved my reading skills. As a young lad I struggled with reading and would actively avoid books and now I had a book glued to my face all the time.

After I read all the technical books I could, I went on to read about other incredible feats of endurance and survival. All of these things gave me the inspiration to keep moving forward. I owe my success to some of these people for sharing their stories. They allowed me to visualise mine. I listened to any podcast that my ears could handle about running and training and heard so many awesome stories.

However, the thing that I struggled with was my nutrition, despite all the books and podcasts. Now I was running longer distances I needed to take in more calories to give me energy. When I was doing half marathon distances or below, I got away without eating. Anything above that, I would need food to keep me going. The thing I was struggling with was trying to fast at the same time. Intermittent fasting suited me because it gave me ultimate control over how I ate, whereas in the past I had had no control whatsoever. Lack of control is how I got to 24 stone, and I didn't want to go back to that at all – I was terrified of going back.

Due to this terror, I did some silly things; I wouldn't eat at all and try to run longer and harder. I quickly learned that this was dangerous. I wouldn't just hit the wall, I would smash into it head first. I would get dizzy and have to sit down. I knew I had to change my mindset to be able to do an ultra. I wasn't 24 stone anymore, and a day of eating while running big hills wasn't going to make me 24 stone once more. I had to get comfortable with eating again. I started to take running gels with me. On my longer runs they would get sickly, and I wouldn't be able to stomach them. I eventually settled on the little bars of malt loaf and Belgian sugar waffles. The sugar waffles were great. Not only did they give me a calorie boost, but they gave me a moral boost. I wouldn't eat them at home because they were full of sugar. I would only eat them while running. They were a little reward to look forward to at certain points in my run. The harder and longer I ran, the more sugar waffles I could eat. Great motivation.

It took me a while, but I got my nutrition under control, and I had my new gear broken in. The one thing I didn't have was a marathon-distance run under my belt. Coach Dave had planned a 40km run broken down into two 20km loops. This would be my last long run and I would taper my training up to race day. The loop started at my front door and went 10km out and 10km back. I would take my water vest and some snacks with me to practise my nutrition strategy. I then left water and extra food at my front door to restock my vest for my second loop.

The run started off great. The first 10km I felt strong and light. The plan was to do each 10km of the 40km in one hour or just over: this was a good pace for me and it would be the strategy we planned to take on the ultra. After my first 10km I was under the hour. This was bad as I knew if I kept up this pace, then later on I would hit the wall. I tried to slow down slightly and continued to eat and drink little and often. I didn't want to eat a lot all at once as it would have sat heavy on my stomach and made me feel sick.

This strategy was working. I got to my front door after my first loop, restocked my water and food supplies and went out for the second loop. When I got to the 25km mark I started to struggle big time. My legs felt heavy, and I was sweating a lot. I had to start to take on more water and salts, so I popped some electrolyte tablets into my bottles. I didn't usually do that because sometimes they could make me feel sick, but I knew I needed them. Thankfully the British weather didn't disappoint and before the 30km mark the heavens opened and blissful cooling rain washed over my hot, flagging body. It rained hard for a good 20 minutes and then the hot sun came back out to dry it up.

As the sun dried my clothes, my nipples began to chafe, and they were chafing badly. I was in big nipple trouble. The salty sweat started to sting my poor raw nipples. This had never happened to me before, but I was glad it was happening now. I made a mental note that, on the day of the ultra, I should tape them up to stop this happening. I kept running despite my troublesome nips. At around the 5km to go mark, I made an executive decision. I was going to run the extra 2km and finish my longest training run as a marathon.

The last 7km of that run was a nightmare. My body was screaming to stop and lie down. My nipples were screaming for me to put them out of their misery. It sounds cheesy, but I thought about where I had come from. I had been 24 stone and now I was a little over 15 stone. I deserved to finish a marathon. It was difficult to do the last 2km as I had to run past my front door. If I listened to my nipples, I would have given in to the allure of stopping. I ignored them and rallied. I found the last bit of willpower inside my body and kept going. My watch beeped, alerting me that I had done it. I had actually done it. I had run a marathon for the first time ever. I almost got emotional. I couldn't believe it. I, Kyle Conway, had run a marathon. Not too long ago if someone had told me I would run a marathon, I would have laughed my cake crumbs in their face and then eaten another cake. I was so happy.

I took a seat on a wall by a petrol station and had a little personal celebration, while my nipples calmed themselves down. As I sat there, my legs started to seize up, and my feet were killing me. A sudden realisation washed over me. I had made a rookie mistake. I had stupidly run 2km past my front door, rather than running 1km past it and then 1km back. Now I had 2km to get home. I stayed sitting there for 15 minutes before attempting the walk home. My legs were stiff, but my nipples were causing me all sorts of bother. It was a long, strange walk home. I was walking as if I had just got off a horse while holding my t-shirt out away from my nipples. I must have looked like a right idiot to everyone driving by, but they didn't know what I knew. ***I had just run a marathon***.

I got home and ran a nice hot bath with loads of Epsom salts. Can you imagine what happened when I eventually submerged my nipples? Yes, the most intense jolts of electric pain radiated through my body from nips to toes. After my bath, Coach Dave called me. He had seen the notification on Garmin Connect that I had done a marathon. He laughed, saying that he knew I would do the extra few kilometres and round it off as a marathon. He asked how I felt, and I explained that I was feeling both terrible and awesome at the same time.

He congratulated me and told me to rest up. The hard work was done, and now we had a few shorter sessions to do to keep loose for the big day. However, as soon as I got out of the bath and had some food, Charlotte forced me to go to Ikea. I didn't actually mind – I was too happy to care. I must have been the happiest man in Ikea, ever. I knew that my end goal was in sight.

People have asked me why I didn't want to do my first marathon at an event to enjoy the atmosphere and get the race bling. I always say that there wasn't one close enough to the ultra marathon date to allow for tapering. However, I wouldn't have wanted to do it any other way. A marathon wasn't the target. It was a milestone to get to my target. Additionally, the confidence and willpower I gained from doing it alone with no fanfare or spectators gave me a massive mental boost.

I should also mention that even though I was the happiest man in Ikea, my nipples were not happy. When dressing for Ikea, I decided to wear my white England rugby top. Halfway around the store in the bathroom section, Charlotte took great pleasure in pointing out the two pink patches that started to appear on my shirt. I was so embarrassed: my nipples were bleeding. I did put in the Ikea suggestion box that they should start selling nipple tape.

When I got home, I moved the coffee table out of the way and started to stretch out my tight, tired legs. I had started yoga in lockdown. I bought a book called *Yoga for Men* and it had several different yoga programmes you could follow. I generally did the recovery programmes and the leg- and hip-strengthening ones. Yoga benefitted me so much: it would allow me to get rid of the niggles and stiff areas after a hard training session. It really helped me after my successful marathon and the next day my legs and hip were in pain but not as much as I had expected. Charlotte reckons that it was walking around Ikea that aided in my marathon recovery. She could be right.

The event was getting closer and closer. I had completed a few shorter-distance slower runs. I did keep getting told off for running too fast and doing too much while I was meant to be tapering, but I felt good and strong. The day before the event came around, I checked and double-checked my kit with military precision. I didn't want to forget anything. I created drop bags of food that would be taken to checkpoints on my behalf by the organisers. This was good as I wouldn't have to carry everything I needed. I did some carb loading and ordered a pizza from a local takeaway. I didn't forget to do my yoga and foam rolling before bed. I was content that everything was prepped for the morning, and I went to bed.

Unfortunately, I couldn't sleep. I started to feel anxious about the run and I let my mind run away with loads of negative scenarios. I couldn't stop my mind thinking. I wanted it to shut up. My big worry was DNFing (Did Not Finish). I had told people I was going to do this run and I couldn't fail now that I had said I was doing it. I kept looking at the hours going by on the clock. Sleep caught me eventually. A deep sleep with no dreams.

Chapter 8
Can I Call Myself an Ultra-runner?

DESPITE THE lack of sleep and getting up twice to pee, I woke feeling relatively okay physically. Mentally, I was worrying. I wasn't worrying about the distance; it was more than that. I was worrying about what I would tell people if I didn't finish. I was worried about the dreaded DNF. I knew that I shouldn't be thinking like this. I tried to visualise myself crossing the finish line victorious, hands in the air with the crowd chanting my name.

I wanted a mental boost, so I put my get-pumped playlist on. Normally, I would save this playlist until the exact moment I needed it in a race. Traditionally, I would run with music, and I had recently upgraded to a swanky pair of bone-conducting earphones. On my long runs, I also like to listen to podcasts. Right now, I needed to be pumped up by loud rock and dance music, not a podcast. I sat there at 5am, eating porridge and leftover pizza. I needed the carbs, listening to electronic dance music and rock to get me in the zone.

After my breakfast of porridge and pizza, I checked my gear again; I didn't want to forget anything. I dreaded getting to the start line and finding that I had forgotten something. Everything was in its place, and I began to load up the car. The first problem hit when I dropped one of my food drop bags. The pre-made electrolyte drinks bottle split and soaked the food in the bag. I prayed this was my only issue of the day and no more were to come. Luckily, I had extra food and an extra bottle. I made another drop bag, making three in total, and a special bag for the end containing a beer.

I woke Charlotte to get ready to drive me to the start line. Charlotte's dad was coming to wait in with the kids as we didn't want to wake them up this early. The plan was for Charlotte to drop me at the start line, drive home, pick the kids up, and at some point, make their way to the finish line in Brighton. Charlotte's dad was five minutes late, and in my already anxious mind, this was issue number two. It didn't matter that I had built in more than enough travel time to cover a 30-minute delay. I needed to relax.

Perhaps listening to my get-pumped tracks at 5am was putting me on edge. Or it could have been the two espressos I had necked. Coffee can be dangerous for a runner sometimes; it can make you run to the toilet. I didn't care at this point. I needed the caffeine. While we waited for Charlotte's dad I must have gone to the toilet about ten times. This was definitely a physical response to how nervous I was. He eventually arrived so I picked up the remnants of my belongings and got in the car.

Driving to the start line, I was quiet and in my own head. I tried not to think about a DNF and tried to visualise myself crossing that finish line. The drive was just over an hour. Even in the car, I needed to keep to my nutrition plan and eat a small amount and sip some water. Have you ever been driving somewhere or travelling to something and not want the journey to end because you were worried about being at the destination? Well, that was me; I didn't want the drive there to end. I kept thinking 20 minutes to go, that's 20 minutes not running. I thought like that all the way: 15 minutes, ten minutes, five, four, three, two, one. The views on the drive gave me a good indication of what to expect on the run. It was mainly lovely green countryside with a sprinkling of monster hills.

We eventually arrived at Christ's Hospital, a grand old school just south of Horsham, where the race would start. It looked awesome. I caught a glimpse of the start area as we were directed into the car park by a man in a hi-vis. I looked: packed. There were so many people there. I noted they all looked relaxed and chatty compared to me. I was tense, quiet and intimidated. I checked my phone before I got out of the car and had several messages of support from my friends and family. This gave me a little mental boost.

I noticed Coach Dave and his partner Paula across the car park. Coach Dave had kindly come to crew me on my first-ever ultra. He had helped to train me and of course wanted to see his handiwork in action and see me achieve my goal. I will be forever grateful for his help and support. Coach Dave had brought his mountain bike and planned to meet me at strategic places and the feed stations to see how I was getting on and provide me with some support.

They came over to the car, and I introduced Coach Dave and Paula to Charlotte, and what would you know? In the distant past, Charlotte and Paula had worked together, despite Paula and Dave now living hundreds of miles away. It really is a small world. Dave asked if I had all my gear: 'Yes, I have.'

'Have you got your salt tablets, as it's going to be hot out there?'

'Yes, I have.'

The next question was issue number three: 'Have you got your sun cream?'

NO!!!!!! I had bloody forgotten sun cream. It was going to be the hottest day of the year, and now

I would be running for hours with no protection. Coach Dave to the rescue. He had brought some with him.

I got my gear, drop bags and newly acquired sunscreen and made my way to registration. I left my crew at the car catching up on old times. I approached the gap in between the buildings where I glimpsed the start area. As I approached, I could hear music pumping, which was a good start; it would get me in the mood. As I made my way through to the main area, I felt quite intimidated. I was surrounded by loads of ultra-lean, ripped, muscular ultra-runners all in cool bandanas, vests, funky colourful headwear and cool shades. They all looked like professionals; they all looked like the David Goggins, the Kilian Jornets and the Courtney Dauwalters of the world.

I quietly registered and showed the marshals my mandatory items, hoping I hadn't forgotten anything. I then wrote clearly on my drop bag my name and number and placed them in the correct checkpoint areas. There were three checkpoints for your personal food and also a number of water stations along the route. I made my way back to the car with my race number, 77. I was struggling to pin it to the bottom of my shirt at the front, so I asked Charlotte to do it for me, and she proceeded to stab me several times. I am sure she was doing it on purpose.

Anyway, number on and with a bleeding stomach, I kissed Charlotte goodbye. She wished me luck and then set off to get the kids and meet me at the finish line. Paula also went off to complete some retail therapy. Coach Dave stayed with me for a while. We had set up a WhatsApp group with all interested parties: friends, workmates, my boss and family. Coach Dave would give them all updates on my progress, how I was feeling, what point in the course I was on, and what time he expected me to cross the line. There were already several messages in the group wishing me good luck and telling me I would smash it. I really hoped I would.

I told Coach Dave I was slightly intimidated by all the other runners as they all looked like super-lean professionals. He said, 'So do you!' I really had forgotten how far I had come. In my head, I was still thinking like a 24-stone man who didn't belong at the start of an ultra marathon. I was a different man now. I was disciplined almost to obsession and probably capable of running 50km. However, the memory of the 24-stone, unhappy person was still somewhere inside me. I have to accept that he will never truly be gone, and I think that's the same for most people who have gone through body transformation.

As I was contemplating what Coach Dave had said, the music went off, and a voice came over the speakers:

'Will the runners please make their way to the starting pen?' This was it! It was GO time. Coach Dave shook my hand and said he would see me out there. We had a quick selfie, and I got into the middle of the pack. I felt maybe I was a bit too far forward and thought about moving back as I didn't want to hold the faster runners up, but I didn't have time.

A loud air horn went off, and we were away. The noise was deafening. There were people shouting and screaming good luck. There weren't even that many people there, but to me, it felt like loads. As soon as I started to run, I began to relax; the anxiety of 'What if I DNF' had left me. It was as if my body went into action mode and out of thinking mode. I felt strong and light. I knew that I was going slightly fast, but I didn't care. This was me so close to achieving what I had set out to do, and I wanted to do it in the strongest way possible.

As we made our way out of the school grounds, the supporters thinned out and we were running through a semi-suburban area past people's homes. You could tell some of these homes cost a bob or two. It was nice to see that even though the people around these homes clearly didn't expect hundreds of Lycra-clad ultra-runners streaming past their family breakfast time, they still shouted words of encouragement, which was a great mood booster. I hoped there would be more of this support to come. It was lovely, quiet and peaceful as we made our way on to a disused railway line that was now a footpath.

At this point, the pack was spreading out, and I had settled in behind a couple of guys who were running at a comfortable pace. Normally, in the races I had done so far, if I saw a person who I thought was running a similar or a little faster pace than me, I would follow them. This was only in races and never a random person on the street. Doing this had pushed me to get personal bests in a few 5km and 10km races – thank you to those unknowing people.

When I did this, I would always be conscious not to get too close and breathe down their necks. There's nothing worse than when you are in the zone and someone else's breathing pattern puts you off and you feel the flecks of their sweat hitting your bare arms and legs. If they got slower or I felt strong, I would overtake them and be on my way. Sometimes they would figure out my game, and put on the afterburners, leaving me in their dust.

As I was minding my own business, keeping my distance from my pace partners, I became acutely aware of someone running very close to my right shoulder. I took a look, and it was one of the professional-looking guys in his fancy shades. I gave him a friendly nod, but he didn't respond. We ran on for a couple of minutes, and I began to feel strange. Why is this guy running so close to me when there's so much open space? I thought maybe he didn't see me nod. So, I did it again and again to give him a friendly alright mate? This time, he responded with a 'Yes thanks.'

Him being so close to me started to annoy me. I thought about stopping, but I decided to run faster. I thought great, I've lost him. He came right back up on my shoulder. Now he was making me angry. I turned and asked why he was running so close to me. Suddenly, he became sort of friendly, but that type of friendly where you can't tell if it's genuine or he's being sarcastic. I decided it would be best not to hit him and get disqualified. Randomly he asked if I had run this race before. He asked what my expected time would be and what other ultras I had done.

I hadn't realised there was an ultra marathon Gestapo. I told him the truth, that this was my first and I wanted to do it in 5hr 30min. He actually laughed at this and said that this would be too hard for me. He told me I had picked a really hard one. He proceeded to tell me that lots of people would pull out of this race. He said due to the hills and it being nearly 20 degrees, not many people would finish. I could sense he was eager for me to ask what ultras he had done. I did resist for a short while, but my politeness took over, and I asked.

I wished I hadn't because he banged on for a good ten minutes about all the ultras he had completed. I was wishing he would just piss off and leave me alone. We came to a small village, and I got my wish. As we got on to one of the village's tarmaced streets, he said what I thought was 'Thanks for the chat.' He then ran off quickly in front of me. However, reviewing the weird interaction, I concluded he had said 'Thanks for the draft.' I realised he was running on my right shoulder. I was blocking the wind and sun for him. I started to get angry and wanted to catch him. I sped up, but he was long gone. Just thinking about what I would have liked to do to him actually made the kilometres go by more quickly. I had never experienced a person like that in a race. Everyone you meet is normally so supportive and encouraging. This guy must have been having a bad day or something.

I was running strongly. I was drinking regularly and eating little and often. I came to the 21km mark where I was meant to meet Coach Dave to report my progress. He wasn't there, so I went on and saw him coming my way. He looked at his watch and exclaimed, 'Jesus Christ, you are going too quick!' I had done a half-marathon in nearly my PB (personal best). I told Dave about the man who annoyed me and that was probably why I had been quick. He promptly scolded me and said we will get him at the finish line. He reminded me that we hadn't even done any of the big hills yet and we were just about to hit a monster. I needed to slow down, or I would blow up before the end. He also pointed out that I had been running downhill for the last 21km and there was now only one way to go.

I told him: 'Message received, slow down and behave yourself.' I carried on running down the road and a marshal directed me on to a small, branchy path. I ran through the branches and the path opened up into the start of the monster hills. There were people walking up. I thought about running up it, but it was too steep. I put my hands on my knees and pushed on as quickly as I could. The sweat was dripping off my nose, and my cap was saturated. I was sweating so much that it was as though I had just gotten out of a swimming pool. I had to stop for a second and have a drink. I couldn't march up the hill, breathe, and drink water at the same time.

I turned around and was suddenly struck by an amazing view of the rolling English countryside. I was amazed at how quickly the view had changed from the bottom to where I was now standing. I took a swig of my water. I nearly vomited there and then. I had been running so long that my body heat and the sun had turned my nice cool water into hot water.

I turned around and looked up. The hill seemed to continue forever. There were ultra-runners everywhere on that hill. They were either marching up, hands on knees, sitting on the ground resting, or looking at the amazing views. I took the opportunity to get my phone out and take a photo. As I was taking photos, I saw I had a number of messages. I opened them up, and there was an audio message from Work Dave. I played the message, and it was dance music, and suddenly a DJ cut in. It was MistaJam on Capital Radio giving me a shout-out. MistaJam was talking about how I had lost nine stone and was doing my first ultra in this heat. I think he called me a machine or something like that. I was so happy that went out across the country. It instantly gave me the energy to carry on up the hill.

I was so happy I recorded a little video thanking Dave and put it in the group chat. I made sure I showed the size of hill I was battling. This hill was a killer. Closer to the top I saw some of the other runners having a lie down. I could understand their plight. I wanted to join them. I also found out this hill was a foul temptress. On a few occasions, I rejoiced that I was at the top only to find that it was a false summit. I knew I was actually at the top when I saw several paragliders jumping off the other side of the hill. I was in awe of the stunningly beautiful scenery around me. I wish I had taken more photos. I couldn't as I was sweating that much my phone screen wouldn't recognise my finger.

I looked at my watch. I couldn't believe how long it had taken me to get to the top. The fun part was to come. I had to run down the other side. I was now over halfway, and just a little further along the top was a checkpoint with one of my drop bags. Thankfully, the checkpoint had some cooler liquids than my body-boiled water. Unfortunately, it was some sort of ginger energy drink. That's just what I needed in this heat and halfway through an ultra marathon, a nice spicy drink. I drank it down all the same and grabbed my drop bag which contained my secret weapon. I pulled out my Belgian sugar waffle and inhaled the thing. I also ate a mini bar of malt loaf and some jelly sweets.

I started to run downhill. This side was so much cooler, and I let gravity take me quicker and quicker down the hill. I hoped the food I had taken on board would be springing into action at the bottom and give me energy to go up the next hill. My wish came true, because as I got to the bottom it certainly did spring into action. It sprang straight out of my stomach and back through my mouth. The spicy ginger energy drink caused an ungodly riot while mixing with the sugar waffle and jelly sweets. It was horrible: all I could taste was ginger and stomach acid. I wiped the chunks of waffle off my face and thought this would catch up with me.

I ran on for a while and came to yet another hill. I took the opportunity to walk up it and tried to get an energy gel into me, but it wasn't working. Anything sugary was making me feel sick. I cursed myself for not sticking to the food and drinks I had practised with. That's ultra running 101, no new kit on race day and no new food and drink. I was stupid, but I needed something cold to drink. I resolved to only drink the hot water in my running pack and try food again after a little while.

I was now about 35km in, and my legs began to feel heavy and tight. I met Coach Dave at the next water station and told him what had happened. He told me I must eat something; it would make me feel better. I tried some crisps, but I couldn't finish the packet. I took some extra salt tablets. There was yet another hill to come just after we crossed a golf course. The golf course was a bit strange, to be fair. The path was narrow, with only room for two people. The golfers were all stood on it and having a chat. They wouldn't move out of the way for any of the runners, and at one point I was forced to step off into a ditch.

I was happy to get past the mean golfers, until I saw the hill I now had to get over. I had become constantly thirsty; my legs were heavy, and ached. All I wanted to do was end this thing. I said to myself if a button appeared to end this race, I would push it and DNF. I pushed on and ran some of the less steep parts of the hill, but I had to walk the steep bits as my quads were beaten up. While I was walking, I had a look around and I couldn't see a single runner. In fact, I hadn't seen a runner for a while. The last one was before the golf course, and they were sitting on a rock eating a banana.

I got it in my head I had gone wrong, taken the wrong path. No wonder those golfers were looking at me funny – if a random sweaty bloke came hobbling past, you would look at them funny. I couldn't have gone wrong: I knew the route inside out. I took out my phone and found the route plan. It showed I was on the correct path, but in my fatigued mind I was convinced I wasn't. It took some willpower not to deviate from what my phone was saying. I carried on forward and eventually, I was passed by a couple of runners. I did my thing and kept up with them as far as I could before they left me in their wake.

Just before the next checkpoint at 40km I saw coach Dave coming towards me, and he had a bottle of cold water. I could see the condensation on the sides. It looked like heaven. I downed it as soon as he gave it to me. He asked about food, and I still couldn't eat. We picked up my drop bag, and I tried to get down some of the sugar waffle but couldn't do it. I said that we were 10km out – I could do it without food. By now, we were getting closer to Brighton, and the route took us past what looked like some old industrial buildings and an old railway bridge.

I had a sudden call of nature and went for a pee. I was shocked at how brown my urine was. The heat of the day and the sickness had really caused me to dehydrate. I ran on and hit the marathon mark. Dave said he would see me closer to the finish line, but as soon as he left, I started to get cramps in my calves. The pain was terrible. It wasn't just one calf, it was both. As soon as I put weight on one, it would immediately contract and not let go. I tried to take on some more salt tablets, but I knew that I had already gone past the point of no return. These tablets wouldn't have much effect. I shuffled on.

The area I was running in was getting busy now. I was running through a built-up housing area along pavements open to the public and roads with cars on them. I found myself wishing I was back in the countryside. People were shouting encouragement and offering me a friendly 'Well done' but I wasn't feeling it, I was in pain and tired. I didn't want people talking to me. I tried to remain pleasant and thank everyone, but I think I may have blanked a few people.

The route took us into a busy park with families and dog walkers. Not more people, exactly what I

24 stone at Simon's wedding to Ultra runner.

At work – the heaviest I have been.

Finishing the Run To The Sea Brighton Ultra.

Having a rest after running 50km over the South Downs.

Running the Why Not Run where I achieved fourth place.

Running my favourite route through Langstone.

Paddle boarding with Simon and my kids.

The weird old church on a hill in Dorset.

Finishing some hard boxing training.

A shot from one of my fights.

Charlotte and I having a well-earned holiday.

Without this bunch of guys, I wouldn't be where I am today.

didn't want. A marshal said that it wasn't far now and that there were no hills left. That felt good. When I got to the exit of the park, Dave was waiting on his bike. He told me there was about 6km to go, and we got this. I ran on the pavement and saw one of the course markers pointing up a hill. I thought, 'What the f**k is that?' I mumbled to Coach Dave that a marshal had told me there were no more hills.

For some reason – probably the pain and dehydration – this made me incredibly angry. I called that marshal all the names under the sun for lying to me. To be fair, he was probably just mistaken or genuinely trying to help. In my fatigued and dehydrated mind, he was the devil. I was well and truly in the pain cave, and Coach Dave kept his distance. He knew exactly what I needed, and that was to work through my issues. Cramp hit again at the top of the hill, and I had to walk for a little bit. It wasn't just my legs cramping; my stomach muscles were too. It was like they were alive and wriggling inside me.

I was now in considerable pain and mental turmoil. I rounded a bend in the road and looked down a long hill. I could see the seafront at the bottom. Down the road there were people milling around outside shops and bars. The wonderful sight of the sea signified that the end was near, but it didn't bring me out of the pain cave. I looked at my watch and saw 3km left. I didn't think this was possible as I could see water. Surely all I had to do was get to the sea.

No, I was wrong. The last part of the run was along the hot and packed promenade. Coach Dave said he was off and would meet me at the end. He went to organise my welcoming party at the finish line. I struggled but got going down the hill. Every step was agony. My calves were tight and ready to burst. My stomach muscles were a close second, they kept spasming. I tried to ignore all the people going about their day, shopping and drinking. I eventually got to the bottom of the hill.

Thankfully I had to wait for the traffic lights to go red before I could hit the last few kilometres; waiting for that green man to show up was bliss. I could hear the finish line as soon as I crossed the road in the distance, the muffled music and a random voice every now and again. I focused on that muffled sound and kept moving. It was hard and slow going. I saw the faster runners who had already finished, walking around with beers and their medals. I wanted that to be me, and there was no way I was going to walk over that finish line.

The blow-up purple finish line came into view. I could see the crowd waiting, and I sped up. I ran the hardest I did in all races. I don't know where that last bit of energy came from because I was basically on my arse for the last 20km. There were so many people cheering and shouting. I spotted my kids at the barrier and gave them a wave, then stepped over the finish line. The commentator called out my name, and a medal was placed around my neck.

Immediately it hit me, I had finished. I had done it. I had achieved what I set out to do. For a few seconds, I felt emotional and as I walked out between the barriers, tears welled up in my eyes. I saw Charlotte, my kids, Coach Dave and Paula, and blinked them away. I sat on the soft grass and they told me how proud of me they were. I didn't get a hug though, because I was dripping with sweat, and I stank. I tried to grab Charlotte for a laugh, but she screamed and ran off.

As I dried off, I moved on to the picnic blanket that Charlotte had put out. I drank nearly two litres of water in one go. I sat there quietly with my water, taking in the conversation and watching other people cross the line. Coach Dave asked me if I was going to do another; I didn't even have to think. 'Of course I am.' We spent a few hours drinking and chatting in the Brighton sunshine. I was slowly coming around to the idea of food when we said our goodbyes to Coach Dave and Paula. I thanked him for his support and for coming to crew me. He will never know how much that meant to me.

Even though I was now dry, Charlotte still made me sit on a towel, and I stank the car out all the way back to Portsmouth. The drive home afforded me some thinking time. I reflected on where I had come from, 24 stone and mentally and physically unhealthy, to a guy who just smashed an ultra marathon. I was happy. I knew I wanted to keep trying for longer distances. I wanted to beat the time I had just set; it had taken me 5hr 55min to get over those hills and complete the 50km. It wasn't quite under the 5hr 30min I wanted, but the course was brutal.

When we got home, I struggled out of the car and barely got up the stairs. I struggled to lower myself into a bath loaded with Epsom salts. Charlotte ordered a takeaway. When it came, I couldn't get down the stairs. My legs were so bad that I sat in bed with my food on my lap. I found I still couldn't eat that much, and the pain in my legs was driving me crazy. It was time to go to sleep, but I found it difficult to nod off.

My head was all fuzzy, like when you get home from a night out and the club has been playing loud music all night. I managed to nod off but woke again, and I was sweating buckets. My sheets were soaking wet. I was that concerned I consulted Dr Google, and it said that this can be normal after intense workouts. I floated back to sleep. When my alarm went off for work, I couldn't even move, and my head was killing me. I felt hungover. I had to call my boss to say I wasn't coming in to work. Thankfully, she had already anticipated this and booked me off. Thank you, Charlotte Morrison. I lay in bed all day, drinking fluids, eating food, and dreaming about what I was going to do next.

Chapter 9

Running into the Future

AFTER COMPLETING my first ultra, I rested for a couple of weeks, only doing yoga and stretching and found that, after a couple of days' rest, I felt normal. I was itching to get back to running, but Coach Dave advised me to rest a bit and let my leg heal. After two weeks, I was champing at the bit to get back outside. A guy I worked with mentioned that he did a run called the Clarendon Marathon. He waxed lyrical about how hard it was and how it had broken him. It sounded right up my street. I went back to my office and did some research. Yes, please, I liked what I saw!

The race was due for later in the year and I booked it there and then. When I got home that night, I told Coach Dave, and we started to work on a plan. I wanted to get faster over longer distances, and this meant longer intervals, tempo runs, and my favourite hill runs. Not only did I book this marathon, but I also booked the Why Not Run, the Great South Run, and, as an extra special treat to finish off the year, the Portsmouth 50km Ultra.

Around that time, I started posting my transformation journey on Instagram. My account began to get a lot of attention and followers. It seemed people were interested in what I was doing. I had messages from all over the world asking for advice and guidance, and it felt good to help people like me. I am not sure how much I actually helped, but it was nice to talk to people about our similar struggles. I felt I wasn't alone, and I hoped they felt like that too. One day, Simon said: 'I bet the local newspaper would be interested in your story.' I contacted them, and a few days later, there was nearly a full page dedicated to me and my progress: it was a real 'local boy done good' story.

I was also a big fan of the *Portsmouth Running* podcast and would listen to it while running or driving to work. I was lucky enough to record a whole episode with the host, Daniel Del Piccolo. I didn't really enjoy doing the podcast, but not because of the host or anything. I felt that I was really nervous and waffled on way too much. To this day, I have not listened to the episode. I can't bring myself to listen to me talking for an hour. I think this is a throwback to when I was big and I couldn't look at myself. I don't think those scars will ever heal.

After that, I was invited to do a little bit of publicity with a local running clothing brand, which was cool. I must admit I was getting a bit of a big head about all this attention. I was then invited on the *Secrets of Weight Loss* podcast to do an episode on my journey. My newfound celebrity status slowed down after this until I got invited on to Capital Radio to talk to a host about his marathon training. This was nerve-racking as it would go live to thousands of people. Then my final bit of stardom came when I got invited with a friend to the premiere of Iwan Thomas's ultra marathon documentary. The documentary was about Iwan running 100 miles over the South Downs. I got to meet Iwan and had a good chat with him; he's a proper nice bloke, and he had actually checked out my story before meeting me.

I was training hard with an aim to get a PB at the Clarendon Marathon and the Great South Run. But first I wanted to see how I would get on in a lap race with an aspiration of doing a 24-hour one. I found two races. One was in July, which was a 6km, three-out-and-three-back over a manageable six hours. This was the Why Not Run, and I found a race for the following year near Stoke that was a 12-hour lapped event. I really loved the idea of at some point being able to run for 12 to 24 hours straight. I booked the six-hour race with the idea I would do it as a test and next year I would do the 12-hour one and finish off with a 24-hour event.

I found the route plan of the Why Not Run and decided to check it out and do some of my training on it. It was a trail that went up the side of a 17th-century stately home called Stansted House to an old tower called Racton Ruins. This was a folly built on a hill in 1766. It's a beautiful area to run, but I quickly assessed that this would be a very difficult race. The first 3km to the ruins was all uphill and the return was 3km downhill. At the time of training, it was wet and muddy, and every time I went, I got filthy. However, despite how difficult I thought it might be, I was the lightest and fastest I have ever been. I felt and looked good. I had a lofty ambition for the Why Not Run, which was to get above 50km in less time than it had taken me to do my previous ultra marathon.

The week of the race rolled around, and I was tapering. I did a few slow 5kms and kept loose on the static bike. I had asked Work Dave to crew me for the run. He said yes and later Charlotte and the kids would take over from him after Charlotte had finished work. I told him all he would need to do was hand me food and drink at the end of each lap. I also told him he would have to massage all of my achy bits. He nearly bit my arm off for the chance of massaging my achy bits!

A couple of days before, I went over what would be in my kit: water, food, salt tablets, gels and a towel. The good thing about the race was I could also bring extra clothing, so once I had sweated through one top, I could change to another. Kit checks and race strategy done, Dave and I waited for the day. The night before, I was nowhere near as nervous as I had been on my first ultra. I actually managed to get a good night's sleep, and I woke feeling as fresh as a daisy.

It was a glorious day. The sun was shining, and the sky was blue. The forecast said it would be the hottest day of the year so far. I thought: 'What's with all my big races falling on the hot days of the year?' Work Dave picked me up from home, and we made our way to the start. When we got there, we set up a nice little spot not too far from the start/finish line, close enough that I didn't have to travel extra distance to get food, drinks and my massages. A lot of people had brought large umbrellas to shelter their little camps from the sun. I blamed Work Dave for not thinking of bringing one.

Before the start, the organisers gave a briefing and paid extra attention to the fact it was a mega hot day. They also said that they had thought about cancelling the event for people's safety. Everyone playfully booed at this comment, and the organisers said we were responsible for our own safety. However, if they saw us suffering, they would pull us out. Cue the playful boos again. We made our way to the start line. It felt good not to have my running pack on. While I was training, I had it on all the time. I didn't need it now I could get what I needed at the end of a lap, but I did carry a hand water bottle.

The hooter went, and we were away. I got as close as I could to the front of the pack as I knew that the paths got narrower the closer we got to Racton Ruins, and there could be a bottleneck. To do this, I had to run quicker than normal for 3km uphill. When it was time to come back down the hill, I was in the front pack. It felt great to be with the skinny vest crew again. I knew it wasn't a sustainable pace, and I would have to slow down soon. When I got to the start/finish line, Work Dave wasn't prepared for me and said I was running too quickly. I swapped bottles, and Dave handed me a malt loaf.

Off I went for my second 3km uphill. I decided to wear a running top that my wife had made for me. It was black with big white letters on the front that spelled out TANK. It was great: everyone was calling me Tank. The marshals were doing it, the other runners were doing it, and even the dog walkers too. I heard 'GO ON TANK,' and 'WELL DONE TANK.' It was a massive confidence booster. This second uphill was more difficult, and I was sweating much more than I normally do because of the heat. I slowed down and took a sip of water every few steps. I was determined not to get dehydrated in this weather. I got to Racton Ruins and turned around to run back down the hill and got talking to another runner about how beautiful Stansted House and Racton were. I really am lucky to live in such a wonderful place.

I got back to the start/finish 12km feeling strong. Dave mentioned that he had a surprise for me when I got back from the next lap. 'How intriguing,' I said to him. I swapped bottles, grabbing a gel this time. It was getting too hot for malt loaf and off I went. On this lap I started to feel a little fatigue setting in. I had also noticed that there didn't seem to be as many runners as there had been at the start. At a split in the path up to the ruins, a nice and jolly marshal was standing there pointing people in the right direction. Every time he saw me coming, he would shout, 'Come on, Tank! I want to see you again on the next lap.' This kept me going every time, thanks mate.

When I got back to the start this time, Work Dave wasn't alone – Coach Dave was there. He had turned up for a bit to see how I was getting on. I thought he was in Manchester, so having him there gave me yet another boost. Without me knowing, Work Dave had organised for Coach Dave to turn up as he was down visiting a friend not too far away. I gave Coach Dave the lowdown on how I was feeling.

He was concerned about the heat and how much I was sweating and told me to go on to the electrolyte drinks ASAP, which I did. Work Dave said that lots of people had already pulled out and stopped because of the heat.

I couldn't spend any more time chinwagging with the Daves. I got back out on my next lap and immediately came across a runner who was puking up. I stopped to see if she was okay. She definitely wasn't okay. I ran the short distance back to the organisers at the start. I grabbed one of them and ran back to the young woman. I was thanked and then released to go back on my way. I kept going slowly, head down, taking sip after sip after sip. This time when I got back to the start, I was feeling the heat. I knew Charlotte would be here soon, so I asked one of the Daves to tip a bottle of water over me and message Charlotte to bring more.

I went back out on the course. This time, on the steeper parts, I walked for a little while. I could no longer tell what position I was in, and I didn't even know what lap I was on. I just kept running and sipping. The calls of 'Tank' kept me going, and the fact that Coach Dave had turned up also made me want to do all six hours. At some point, Charlotte and the kids turned up to relieve Work Dave, but he ended up staying for the whole six hours.

I went off again slowly. The heat was getting to me, and I wanted to stop. The constant up and down was killing my quads. I had no idea how many laps I had done. I was trying to work it out in my head, but I couldn't. I made a deal with myself that if I was over a marathon, I would stop. When I got back to the start, everyone was having a nice sit-down picnic style, and my drink bottle wasn't made. With the heat and pain in my legs, I sulked while I waited for them to be mixed. I asked how many laps, they told me a number, and I thought: 'God, I am way behind where I thought I was.'

I only found out at the end that they purposefully shaved off a lap so that I would keep going. I knew we were getting close to the six hours and couldn't quite add it up in my head. I went back out and suspected they were lying to me, which in my state annoyed the hell out of me. This lap was a killer, and there weren't many runners left. I had to walk up some of the hill until I saw the jolly marshal who was now calling me 'Super Tank' because I wouldn't stop. I got to the ruins and needed to sit down.

I was now in my own head and the negative talk started. I was telling myself I couldn't do a 24-hour event because I couldn't even do a six-hour. I stumbled back down the hill content that I was calling this my last. When I got back to the team at the start, they were all animated and said if you go back out now, you can get another lap in. Just one more lap, 'GO! GO NOW!' Miserable and hot, I shuffled off back up the hill. The constant running on the rocky path was killing my feet, and I decided to run-walk on any amount of grass possible. For the pleasure of walking on the grass, I nettled my legs multiple times. The jolly marshal was shocked to see me again and said he thought I wouldn't have come back out. I just wanted this to end. I shuffled back down the hill and crossed the line with only about ten minutes left of the event. If you got caught out on a lap after the six hours was up, that lap wouldn't be counted.

I crossed the line and couldn't move. I lay on the grass between the start line and where the Daves and Charlotte were sitting. Eventually, they coaxed me over with a cold bottle of orange juice. I sat there, glad it was over and with an empty and exhausted mind. The end buzzer went to signify the six hours was up. Coach Dave said, 'Go ask the organisers how many laps and what position you came in.' I dragged myself over to the timing mat and the guys on the computers. In the end, I had done eight laps and 48km, but my Garmin was a little over 50km. Although I had not got the distance I wanted, I had come in fourth place, beating many of the skinny-running-vest crew.

THE SWITCH

I was ecstatic, and amazed by how everyone was really happy for me. I needed to rest but most of all I needed to cool down. I thanked both Daves for coming to crew me. Their presence had really kept me going. I thanked them for lying to me to keep me on the course. Without them, I wouldn't have achieved fourth place. On reflection, I think that the weather played a big part in my placing in this race. The heat definitely knocked out a lot of the competition. I believe on a cooler day I would have been down the pack. Still, it's nice to get a fourth now and then.

I went through my traditional recovery when I got home: ice bath, hot bath, yoga, water, and a massive takeaway. The night of a big run or a big training day, I find I can't sleep and my legs twitch and spasm. After this race, I slept like a baby. However, in the night I must have been sweating buckets. When I woke up, my sheets were soaking wet, and I had the mother of all headaches. I still hadn't hydrated enough. That morning, despite my throbbing head, I went to book the 12-hour race that I had spotted up near my home city of Stoke-on-Trent, but it was sold out. I should have booked when I first saw it, but I put it out of my mind and cracked on.

I continued to push my training sessions as hard as I could. I felt strong and I knew I would get my marathon PB. Then disaster. On one of my long runs,

I began to feel that old familiar piriformis pain in my bum cheek. I did what every good runner does and ignored it. I had not learned my lesson from the first time. I kept training and pushing it until I had trouble walking. It was time I had to come clean and admit I was injured. Coach Dave immediately called me and sent me to the physio. They gave me the bad news. I had to stop running and let it settle down. I had been overtraining again.

As I write this, I know that I should have stopped as soon as I felt the pain, but at the time I thought I could train through it. I struggled with not running for a while and became irritable. It was clear that I had become totally obsessed with training and managing my eating, and, I guess, the psychological effect of fearing that I would go back to what I was.

At least I had my stretching, and I was allowed to hit the gym as long as I did no impact work. I mainly used the stationary bike, which gave me no pain. I did some upper-body weights, mainly chest and shoulders. My physio told me to use the cross trainer but that did hurt, so I skipped that one. While I was injured, I lost a good few weeks of training and some key long runs. By the time I slowly got back to running, I was only a few weeks from the Clarendon Marathon. I had missed my big long run. I had not tested a nutrition plan, but I had remembered not to drink anything spicy or run the risk of sickness. If I hadn't been as tight with money as I am, I would have pulled out of the race. But I had paid my money and if I had to walk the whole way, I was doing it.

Before the race, I managed to squeeze in a few slow, long runs which felt okay. My bum cheek was still tight, but I carried on regardless. Egotistically, I thought to myself, how hard can it be? I have already completed two ultras. The day of the race came around, and I made my way to Winchester Park and Ride, where the runners would get picked up and taken to the start. I parked the car, grabbed my gear, and made my way to the pickup point. It was a nice, clear day. The weather forecast predicted warm, sunny weather. No worries, I had run in warmer conditions.

I got the familiar pang of anxiety and feeling out of place when I saw the other runners getting on the coach. It's a strange thing really. I don't think I will ever get rid of that feeling of not quite fitting in. I made my way to the back of the coach, as I did during my school days. I could be naughty at the back of the bus where the cool kids sat. An older gentleman approached, possibly in his late 60s, and sat next to me. So much for being naughty, I thought. As the bus pulled away, we began to chat. I was surprised to find out he had run this race multiple times in his younger days. He told me back in the day he was an ultra-runner and ran many 100-mile races. He said these days he could just about manage 50km.

Bloody hell, I thought. I hoped I would be casually knocking out 50km at that age. We discussed my running experience, and I showed him some photos. I noticed a beaming smile come across his face, and he asked if I was the guy on the *Portsmouth Running* podcast. I shyly said yes, and he congratulated me on my transformation. This was the first time I was recognised in the wild. I told him about my injury and lack of training. He gave me confidence, saying that I shouldn't have lost too much fitness since my ultra and that I should bag this easy.

Great! I thought. His confidence made me think I am sure to smash it. We got to the start line at a village hall. Registration was inside, and my new friend and I went to get our kit checked and get our numbers. The hall was packed, and you could hardly move. The organisers announced that anyone who wanted to start early could do so. All we had to do was make our way to the start. I jumped at the opportunity. I wanted to get out of that packed hall, and the sooner we got going, the sooner I could finish. My new friend said he would start a bit later as he wanted a bacon roll first. He said he would see me out there. I cockily thought: 'No chance.'

I made my way to the start line. I was one of four people who wanted to go early. The man at the start checked my number and said, 'Off you go.' No buzzer, no hooter, no whistle, just off you go. I was glad I had started early. It was a good strategy to get some kilometres under my belt while it was slightly cooler. The four people I started with stayed together for the first 10km and then I found myself pulling off ahead. I thought this was easy, no problem.

Then I hit the hills, and it was grim. My legs became heavy, and I couldn't keep any momentum. I felt like I couldn't catch my breath. I was shocked at how much endurance I had lost while injured. I had to make a deal with myself to walk up the hills, then run the downs and flats. At the start of the race, the hills were open with no shade. I had forgotten sun cream again and had to use a buff to stop my neck burning. It was hard going. Then people began to stream past me, running strongly.

This knocked my confidence and I just wanted to get it done. As I was going up one particularly grim hill, I felt a tap on my shoulder, and it was my friend from the bus. I told him I was suffering. He smiled and told me he would get me a beer at the end. Then he was off, like he was floating up the hill. I was envious of him, and I felt low mentally. I thought about DNFing. I had not done this before, but I was really thinking about it. I planned that at the next water station I would jack it in and wait for the car to take me to the finish.

When I arrived there, I couldn't bring myself to do it. I just sat for a while, ate a banana, and sipped on some water. I hobbled off again with a new determination to get to the end. I convinced myself my second wind would come shortly. I managed to get another 10km running non-stop, but that killed me. I had nothing left in the tank. The course took me through a long forest area and I had a little sit down on a log to recalibrate. I worked out I had about 10km to go and if needs be I could walk it.

This was the hardest 10km of my running career. My mind had gone. I had let the negative thoughts win. I didn't want to be there anymore. I had started the race thinking I would do it easily, and now I was telling myself I had no business running at all. My mental state was the worst it had been in any race. It was worse than when I was 24 stone, running in the dark.

I came out of the forest on to a village road. I knew the finish line was close, but I couldn't bring myself to run. I walked through a small crowd cheering and clapping, and crossed the line. I felt bad as I collected my medal. I felt I didn't deserve it because I had walked. I was disappointed in myself. I had finished this marathon slower than I did my ultra marathons. There were stalls everywhere, a real village fair-type atmosphere. People were eating, drinking and listening to a band on stage. I didn't care. I just made my way to the shuttle buses taking people back to the park and ride. I sat waiting for a good 20 minutes before we set off. Thankfully, only a couple of people got on my coach. Everyone else was still enjoying themselves.

I spent the next few days sulking like a child. I was being way too hard on myself. I was ignoring the positives that had come out of the Clarendon Marathon. I had completed a marathon with minimal training, and my injured piriformis was absolutely fine. But it took me a few days to realise this and get over myself.

Chapter 10
Running into the Future, Part 2.

IT WAS time to get my focus off my miserable Clarendon Marathon performance and get ready for the Great South Run. Before this, I received a present so thoughtful and nice I nearly cried. Charlotte had taken my Run to the Sea Brighton race number, medal, and a printed photo of me crossing the finish line. She had them put it in a presentation box. It was lovely, and I put it in my office. I look at it every day.

Charlotte had also purchased the official coffee mug from the Run to the Sea Brighton organisers. The mug showed the route, my number and my time. It quickly became my favoured coffee mug. However, one afternoon while working on this book, I heard Charlotte shout 'shit'. While she was putting away the washing-up, she accidentally smashed the handle of the mug. She said it was an accident, but I think she did it on purpose because it didn't match her expensive new pink Next mugs!

I was back to normal with no injuries and continued my training sessions around the Portsmouth area. With Coach Dave's help, we were concentrating on getting faster for the Great South Run. We were aiming for speed. My training for this race went well. I felt confident and well prepared. The day of the run came around. I was due to get a lift from Havant to Portsmouth. My lift cancelled on me at the last minute. I couldn't take the car. Most of the roads around Portsmouth were closed for the race. I thought about the train or a taxi. The train would be packed, and a taxi would cost money. So I decided to ride my bike the 16km to the start line. I thought I would take it slowly, and it would be a nice warm-up and cool-down for the race. Plus, it had the added bonus of not having to wait in traffic or queue for a train. I made my way to the start line on my bike and was surprised to see loads of runners doing the same. I was in good company. I recorded the ride on my Garmin, and as soon as it uploaded to Garmin Connect, Coach Dave was on the phone asking if I had really just ridden my bike to the start line.

This was like no other race event I had entered. The atmosphere was awesome. Southsea seafront had been transformed into a sea of cheering spectators, creating a carnival vibe. There was music and charity cheer squads; they turned a race into a party. There seemed to be bags of camaraderie with all the runners. I chatted with strangers about how cool the whole atmosphere was.

I made my way to the start situated on the seafront. The course would take us around the city of Portsmouth and finish back on the seafront. I had spent years living in Portsmouth and had never bothered visiting some of the sites that this race passed. It was a really good advertisement for the city.

The race started, and it took a couple of minutes to get to the actual start line. As soon as I got over the line, I hit that button on my Garmin and ran hard. The only place that we all got bunched up was near the historic dockyard. I had to slow my pace as there was no way to sneak through the crowds. Even though I had ridden my bike the 16km to the start line, I was flying. I felt strong. The thing that kept me going was the sheer amount of support on the whole course.

The races I had done before this were long trail runs through the countryside where there's no place for supporters. These types of runs can be quite lonely, especially when you are in the pain cave. There's no one there to pull you out of the cave. There were plenty of people here that could help me out of the pain cave if I slipped in. Another great thing about the Great South Run is that it is flat. There are no interruptions through having to walk up steep hills. Also, I didn't have to bother with a nutrition strategy.

I remember the route went up by the police station and then looped around on itself. The earlier runners were coming towards me, and everyone was shouting words of support. I decided to set myself a little challenge and picked a man wearing a dinosaur shirt to catch when I eventually got to the turning point. He was a good half of a kilometre in front of me, but I went for it. I started to pump my legs, and I caught him just as Southsea came into view again. I was running hard, and my legs were turning like pistons. My body felt great, I was breathing hard but I had no pains or aches.

As I was getting to the point where I was to turn back on to the seafront to run the last few kilometres back, I saw some of my old rugby friends, and it was good to run with them for a few minutes. I couldn't hang around reminiscing though, so I said my goodbyes and ran on. This really was a lovely flat course that took you past some historic sites, and you were lured into the loveliness. Until the last few kilometres. As I ran around the corner to get back on the seafront, I was smashed and pushed back by the prevailing winds coming off the sea. During some gusts, it was like running through treacle.

As I got closer to the finish, I used what was left in the tank and sped up. I wanted to finish strong.

RUNNING INTO THE FUTURE, PART 2.

The support at the finish line was awesome. I felt as I imagined a professional runner must feel as they cross the finish line. I used my last bit of energy to cross the line in 1hr 25min. Crossing that line was pure elation – I was completely taken by the atmosphere. I was met with a nice shiny medal and a cool goodie bag.

I had got quicker and even managed to negative split the race in two. I met some friends from work and grabbed a bite to eat and a beer. I stayed to watch and support other runners crossing the finish line, which I had never before felt compelled to do at a race. Then I rode the 16km home on my bike. It was probably the slowest bike ride I have ever made, but I was beaming with joy over what I had just experienced.

This race gave me the taste of those big runs that you see on TV, like the London Marathon or one of the other big city marathons. I really enjoyed the party atmosphere, and people are right when they say that atmosphere can give you extra energy. I really recommend the Great South Run to anyone.

After the run and my bike ride home, I decided to use a new toy that Charlotte had bought me – an ice bath! I had been using it recently over the summer and found it really helped me recover. I would use the ice bath as soon as I got back from a training session, still hot and sweating, and loved it. As we got into October, it began to get colder and harder to find the willpower to get in it. It turns out I am now a fair-weather ice-bather. Anyway, I felt like I didn't need to rest, but Coach Dave advised me to, and so I did what I was told. It was hard because I was itching to get back out.

After a few days' rest, cutting it short by a couple of days – don't tell Coach Dave – I was back at the training. I had one more planned race, and that was the Portsmouth 50km in December, a nice local ultra marathon with a Christmas vibe. My training went well again. I was performing better intervals and better tempo runs. I was eating up the miles on my long runs. My body was a machine and never felt as good as it did when I was notching up the miles.

I would get up early on a Saturday morning, have a cup of coffee, and hit the road. I started to use these long runs to explore my local area. I would quite often grab my old Ordnance Survey map of Portsmouth and West Sussex, plot a route, and just go. I loved going through the back roads and woods towards Chichester. I loved running along the shore from Portsmouth to Emsworth. There was so much beautiful scenery to see and I soaked it all in.

The day of the race came, and I was dropped off at Castle Field in Southsea. The route seemed easy, just following the shoreline as far as the beach on Hayling Island. You would then turn around and come back. The race got off well and I found myself wishing that I had worn more clothing as I was really cold. In fact, I was so cold that I was shivering. I started to feel warm and stop shivering at about 10km in. 'It is December after all,' I thought.

The route took us to a small grassy area by Eastern Road before putting us back on the path that runs along the shore. The problem was that there were multiple paths to take and no marshal or signage to direct you which way to go. This left about 40 ultra runners scratching their heads on which one to choose. Someone got out a phone to look at the map, but it wasn't clear which path to take. An older and bolder runner picked a path and said this one, and pretty much all of us followed. What do you know, it was the wrong path. We spent a while running around in circles until we eventually found the right direction.

Later I found out that the marshal had stood in the wrong place and never once thought it was strange that they hadn't seen any runners. This little mistake had added 1.5km to the 50km, making it a nice round 51.5km ultra marathon.

My nutrition was on point. My Belgian sugar waffles and small malt loaf bars became my go-to proper food. I had a few gels also for that quick energy. I ate and drank little and often, not letting myself feel hungry or thirsty. I ran the Eastern Road part of the race strongly and continued this through the Farlington marshes and hit the famous Hayling Billy Line, a disused railway line that used to run from Havant to Hayling Island, which is now a lovely nature path. Just before getting to the turnaround point on Hayling beach, I started to feel strange. I felt light-headed and a bit floaty. I thought this was odd, as in training I had smashed this distance no problem.

With my vast medical knowledge of nothing, I deduced that maybe my blood sugar was down. I walked a couple of minutes while eating a sugar waffle and then ran on, and it cleared pretty quickly. I carried on running to the halfway turnaround. Here I saw the guys from the *Portsmouth Running* podcast, and we had a quick chat. I filled up my bottles and went on my way back to where I started. I was feeling pretty comfortable at the 25km point and thought I would try and give it a bit more speed and stepped it up a little.

As I made it back off Hayling Island, I started to think about what I wanted to do next. I allowed my mind to daydream for a good few kilometres and I wondered how much further I could go. I thought about perhaps one of the 24-hour lap races where you keep going for as many laps as possible. I also fancied a triathlon, which involves swimming, cycling and then running. I had watched a few videos of Ironman events and the crazy ones like the Celtman and the Norseman. I wanted a bit of that action.

RUNNING INTO THE FUTURE, PART 2.

As I kept running, I realised that when I got to the end of Eastern Road, I still didn't know the correct path to take, and I hoped there was a marshal. I found myself getting anxious about it. I wanted to know which way to go. It was a strange feeling that I put down to running hard for a long time. I slowed down for my final sugar waffle and a banana.

When I got to the part of the course I was worrying about, there were now signs and a marshal – goodness knows why I started to worry and panic. The course took us back on to the seafront, and this time there was a cool breeze, unlike the in-your-face gusts at the Great South Run. The end of the course had us running through Southsea Castle, which was a good boost of energy as it was full of visitors and tourists, and they were all so supportive.

I crossed the line in 5hr 25min, much quicker than my first 50km. This time I didn't have any troublesome hills, but I did have an extra 1.5km. I was happy with that. I had done some hard races and intense training this year. Waiting for me at the end were my kids and my father-in-law, Paul. I was handed a pack of Bounties as a treat and a nice big cold bottle of water. We made our way home and I set about my usual recovery activities and started on the Christmas chocolates.

Chapter 11

New Year, New Me!

WE SPENT Christmas in Stoke with some family and I only went for a few runs. By the time I got home to the south coast for New Year, I felt guilty for all the food and drink I had shovelled into my face. I spent most of the period between Christmas and New Year looking at races I could compete in. However, I started to feel bored with running – I had done so much training and so many events in 2021 that I felt I needed something different. I found a duathlon – running, cycling and then running again – for February 2022 and decided to book it.

I didn't have a road bike, but I thought it would be an easy process picking one up. I needed a road bike if I was going to fulfil my triathlon and Ironman aspirations. It wasn't easy at all; it was a nightmare to find a good bike. I'd never had a road bike before, because I didn't think those thin tyres were designed to hold a 24-stone beast. After multiple trips to bike shops I realised I couldn't bring myself to pay hundreds of pounds for a bike I might only use once. I started to look on second hand sites. I found an XL Giant bike on Gumtree. It looked perfect. I travelled to a private school in Chichester to pick it up. The man I got it from seemed to be minted. He said that he was selling this one as he had the same bike in his New York home. The bike seemed almost new. He had taken good care of it. I had a quick ride, and I snapped it up. He also gave me a massive box of accessories. It was a proper bargain.

Close to the end of January we were invited to a white-collar boxing event in Southsea. One of Charlotte's friends was fighting another woman for charity. I am a big boxing fan and like to watch all the big fights, but I had never really thought about white-collar. I went along not expecting much, but the venue was glamorous, and the booze was flowing. We had a table quite close to the ring, and I could feel the action.

I was captivated from the beginning and I found myself dodging punches in my seat. There were some awesome fights, and I got right into the action. The night ended with Charlotte's friend winning, and a few more pints later, it was time to go home. As we stood about to leave, I saw the list of people who were allocated to sit at that table. I picked it up and read the line at the bottom: 'If you like what you see and want a chance to dance under the lights, then go to this website.' I drunkenly thought I just might.

I couldn't get the thought of giving boxing a go out of my head. I started to do some research. I first went to the website that I had found at the white-collar event. It showed a boxing gym in Leigh Park, a suburb of Havant that is considered by some to be a rough area. I started to follow the gym's Facebook page and watched their videos. Some of them showed proper monsters going to war and others showed normal people like me having their moment under the lights.

This gave me confidence: I was a normal bloke. It also looked like a proper boxing gym and I was glad to see that it wasn't a national white-collar boxing organisation. I decided I wanted to do this, so I messaged the gym owner on Facebook, a guy called Bill. I didn't get a reply for a couple of days. This left me on tenterhooks: the longer I had no reply the more I wanted one. I think that is one of my character traits – if there is something I want to do, I research it obsessively. Then when I make my mind up, there is no deviation, and I want to move quickly.

I went back to work still waiting for a reply from Bill. Work Dave and I were discussing the events we wanted to do next. I told him I still had the ambition to do a 24-hour running event, 100km ultra and the big one, an Ironman. I also told him that I had fallen out of love with running slightly and I wanted to do something different. I told him that I had booked a duathlon and that I couldn't shake the idea of boxing and fighting at a white-collar event.

Work Dave is a seasoned army veteran with much experience of fighting and, out of pure friendly concern, tried to talk me out of it. This made me want to do it more, so I jumped back on Facebook and sent Bill another message. While I was waiting for a reply, Work Dave asked if I had at least talked it through with Charlotte, which I had not. I didn't even think for one second she would be against the idea, so I promised I would tell her that night.

Later in the afternoon I got a reply from Bill saying 'No worries.' It showed a timetable of three sessions a week, the cost and what gear I needed to bring with me. That night I went home and told Charlotte my plan and she was well up for it. She's always been supportive of my extreme endurance pursuits. She either loves me a lot or really wants my life insurance money!

There were a couple of days before my first session, so I went about the business of buying my gear. It was easy enough to get the gloves and hand wraps that protect your hands inside the gloves. However, it was hard to find a comfortable pair of boxing shoes that were size 12 and wide. The size 12s I tried in the big brands were way too tight and thin, so I had to settle for a pair of size 14 shoes that made me look like a clown. To be fair, they fitted, and I could easily move around in them.

Gear purchased, I went about learning how to wrap my hands correctly. I watched numerous YouTube tutorials and had no problem wrapping my left hand but when I came to do the right, I was a mess. I got so wound up with it that I went back to the sports shop and brought a pair of glove-style wraps that I could slip my hands in without embarrassment.

The day of my first training session came and I was quite nervous. I drove to the gym and found a parking space where I sat battling some trepidation. I went through a small door, up some narrow stairs and into a hallway. The hallway was between two larger rooms that contained a ring each and several punching bags of various sizes. The larger room also had an assault bike, skier and a rowing machine.

I waited in the hallway with a group of mainly men with one or two women. It was quite intimidating feeling like the new guy. No one really talked to me, but I also kept myself to myself. The kids' session that was taking place in the large room finished and they ran down the stairs in good spirits. Then from the office a couple of the coaches came filing out, one shouting 'Right you lot, get in, get ready and shadow box, come on, warm up.' I thought that must be the boss man Bill. I went over to introduce myself and he said my Instagram handle, 'killingitwithkyle', so I knew he had checked me out. He shook my hand and told me to just do what the others do, and the coaches would help. I got my easy-to-wear wraps on my hands and began to shadow box. I watched the others keenly and tried to copy them. It felt strange and unnatural to move like this. I can't imagine how awkward and stiff I must have looked. I often feel awkward in social situations, but this was another level.

As a bloke you can't help but size other people up and I would call myself a people-watcher. So, I watched the coaches interact with the people training and was encouraged to see that they were friendly and helpful. There was some banter flying between the regulars and coaching staff, but it was only light-hearted ribbing. There were one or two other newbies, and we got taken into the other room to do some pad work. I suspected it was to see what we had in terms of ability. I was still feeling awkward, like a fish out of water.

One coach turned up late and walked into our room and, as luck would have it, I knew him from an old job. He was a guy called Mike, and he came over to say hello. This made me feel a lot better. After our separate newbie session, we got sent back into the main room where everyone was now doing three-minute circuits around all the bags and exercise machines. There were a couple of regular boxers in the ring sparring. Every now and then the people who were sparring changed and I noticed that no newbies were called up, which was probably a good thing because we would either get our arses handed to us, or go dangerously out of control. The coaches were doing the right thing and assessing our ability and commitment first.

The session went on and while I was on the bags the owner, Bill, was walking around and giving people advice on how to improve their stance and power. He came up to me a few times and said I needed to snap my punches, be quicker. Then he would show me, but I still had no idea how to do it. The session carried on and it was the most I have ever sweated in my life. I was dripping. Right at the end everyone stopped what they were doing and found a space. Then one of the coaches led us through a killer abs workout, where we had to lie on our backs and raise our legs off the floor at an angle and keep them there. This went on for ages: my core muscles were on fire. Thankfully it ended and I went to get my stuff and a well-earned drink of water. Just as I was leaving Bill asked if I had enjoyed it, which I said 'Yes' to, and then asked if I would be back next session and again I replied 'Yes.'

Driving home, I reflected on the session. The coaches were all great, friendly and helpful. However,

NEW YEAR, NEW ME!

I felt awkward and out of place. I knew deep down that this was a 'me' problem and I told myself I probably hadn't looked as bad and awkward as I had felt. Physically after the session I felt great, I could feel that I had used muscles that I never used while running. I got home, had a bath full of Epsom salts and then did some yoga before bed.

The next morning the delayed onset muscle soreness (DOMS) had well and truly kicked in. My arms and shoulders were tender, but my core was worse. If I twisted in a certain way it would cause pain to shoot up my abs. It caused a rush of air to leave my body with a strange, pained sound. I sounded like an 80-year-old man. When I got to work, I filled Work Dave in on how it had gone. I told him that my core and shoulders were a mess, and I needed to get them used to the impact of punching something hard over and over again for an hour. He asked if I was going back and I said 'Yes,' but inside I still wasn't sure. I didn't want to feel like a fish out of water again and it is easier to hide from those situations.

The next day there was another boxing training session. I woke in the morning, and the DOMS was still kicking about so I spent nearly an hour stretching and massaging every bit of me before work. I really wasn't sure if I was going back. Then at work we had a big customer meeting where it was announced that

I was now a boxer (thanks Dave). That was it now, I had no choice – I had to go back that night. Too many people knew and now the main customer at work knew what I was doing. It would have been more awkward not to go back.

The second time I went in the gym, I got glimmers of recognition from some of the guys I had trained with the session before. It was nice – nods and fist bumps were exchanged. We all went into the big room and started shadow boxing to warm up. Bill walked in and shouted my name with a couple of others and said: 'Shadow box in the ring.'

Bloody hell, I was happier just plugging away in the corner; now everyone could see me. The session went pretty much the same way as the previous one. I gave it my all and was dripping with sweat. On the punch bags I was still being told I needed to snap more, throw the jab out quicker. I made an effort to talk to some of the guys; we swapped names and stories. A few of them asked if I would be fighting in the next show in the summer. I told them I had only just started, so didn't think I would be ready.

One of the coaches said: 'Don't worry about that, we will have you ready. Plus we wouldn't put you in against anyone out of your league.' I opened my big mouth, letting my ego get the better of me, and agreed that I would be up for it. After the session I was pretty much the same way as the last. Straight afterwards I was fine but, in the morning, I had terrible DOMS. I told Charlotte I would be fighting in the summer and she was shocked that it was so soon. She asked me if I thought I would be ready. Again, all ego and bravado, I said 'Of course I will,' but in my head I didn't know. 'I will just go with the flow.' Once again, she supported me! Definitely getting closer to that life insurance pay out ...

I went to the third weekly session on a Saturday morning. This session was much quieter, and I got some one-on-one time with a coach called Lee. Lee is one of the nicest guys I have ever met, but an animal in the ring. Lee boxed at a very high standard and represented his country. He did some pad work with me and gave me confidence, telling me I had a powerful punch.

I got a lot out of the one-on-one sessions. This was the session when I first did some light sparring. I got in the ring with a coach called Rob and he went really easy on me. Rob didn't hit me hard but kept telling me to hit him. At first, I didn't want to, I liked the guy. Then after the second round I went to my corner and Lee told me the idea behind what we were doing. This was training to get over the fear of punching someone. He said I need to get used to hitting someone even if I like them. Rob had chosen to get in the ring, and he wanted to get hit.

I understood what Lee meant and as the buzzer went, I hit Rob. As soon as I connected, I thought, 'Shit, he's going to knock me out,' but he didn't, he said: 'GOOD! Now do it again.' I got out of the ring after my three rounds and felt amazing. I had survived; albeit I hadn't been hit hard. I watched the first round of the next spar, then got on the punch bag circuits. On each bag you did different combos such as jab, jab, punch or uppercuts. My feedback at the end of the session was good but there was that word again: 'SNAP your punches.' Determined to snap my bloody punches, all weekend I watched YouTube tutorials and old fights to see how the pros did it.

The next boxing session was full again as it was a weeknight, but I spent some time doing pad work with Mike. I was trying to put the YouTube tutorials into practice and do what Mike told me. All of a sudden when I punched the pad Mike was holding, it made an almighty snapping noise. I instantly knew I had got the snap. Mike said 'That's it,' and I kept practising and when Bill came around, he said 'You've got it now.' We had a few more sessions before we started to spar properly and I sparred with some good lads with skills beyond mine. This was the only way to learn.

In my life I have only had one or two bad nosebleeds, and they were down to getting tackled in rugby. However, I got my worst nosebleed sparring with one of the coaches. I had a problem when sparring, as I kept rocking my jab arm up and down. I don't know why. I often didn't know I was doing it, but doing it caused my jab arm to fatigue. When my arm was fatigued, I dropped my hand away from my face, leaving it unguarded, and the coach bopped me square on the nose.

It wasn't even that hard, but I felt wet all over my mouth and beard. I instinctively licked my tongue out and tasted the coppery thickness of my own blood. I carried on for a bit but was told to get out of the ring so that I didn't get the canvas bloody. I went into the toilets, and my nose was in free flow. I have never had one this bad. It took ages to stem the flow and then I couldn't spar for the rest of the session. The worst bit was that it kept bleeding for days and if I got the slightest of touches on the nose it would go again. Later someone said it might have been broken. I am not too sure but if you look closely my nose is slightly bent, which it wasn't before.

There were only a couple of other heavyweights in our gym, so I ended up sparring with the coaches a lot. One of the guys I did spar with often was Lewis, a good bloke and we were evenly matched, which was good.

As we got closer and closer to the summer, I started to feel worn out. Strangely, in the heat I was always cold. Sometimes it felt like my core was shivering, as if I had internal tremors. I started to feel dizzy while at rest and my Garmin watch would give me 'abnormal heart rate' warnings. My heart rate was too slow. Once after a heavy training session, I came home and got ready to go out for a meal with Charlotte and the kids. I drove us to the pub where we were meeting friends, and for the life of me I could not park the car. I was trying to reverse it into a diagonal space, and I just couldn't get the angle right. I had so much brain fog and confusion I just couldn't do it. The atmosphere in the car made it worse because Charlotte and the kids went from laughing at me to genuine concern. I left the space and parked in a normal one, nose first, to save any embarrassment from trying again.

I was unnerved. For the whole meal I sat there worrying whether I had a concussion or something. The next day I was fine, so I put it down to over-training and not eating enough. I had a few days off from doing anything and ate like a king, which seemed to sort me out. I took it that I should focus my training and ensure I was getting adequate rest and recovery. I stopped my cycling and gyming so much in between big training sessions. This seemed to work, and the brain fog and dizziness went away, but I continued to struggle with always feeling cold.

Training in the gym was getting more intense as we got closer to fight night. We were sparring a lot more and doing new sessions like 'shark tank', where I would be in the ring for five rounds sparring with a fresh opponent every round. It was hard and exhausting work, but I loved every second of it. I look back now and I can see how far I had come – from the quiet and intimidated guy who first walked into the gym, who had felt awkward and stiff shadow boxing, to now a more confident and capable fighter. The lessons that were being taught to me in the boxing gym were beneficial in my normal life as well. The discipline and resilience required in boxing is extremely valuable in everyday life. If you can get in a ring in front of people, knowing you are going to get punched and you must punch back, there is not a single situation that you can't deal with.

It was now summer 2022, and we were back to the beach as normal. Me, Simon, the wives and kids would rock up after work with paddleboards and a BBQ and stay there until late evening. But my recurrent cold feelings were getting worse; I couldn't spend more than a couple of minutes in the sea before I started to shiver violently. I had started to lose feeling in my thumbs any time I got chilly, and my fingers would go white, as if there was no blood in them. I went to the doctor and explained my issue. The doctor wasn't too concerned – he said that the coldness was because I had lost a huge amount of weight and my numb thumbs were due to punching people, pads and bags repeatedly. He told me to stop boxing for a while and my thumbs would be okay. 'No chance,' I thought. 'I have a fight coming up.'

I left the doctor's feeling confident that I had nothing major wrong with me and vowed that I would rest after my fight. Training was reaching a peak in the gym before we tapered off for fight night. It peaked with a session where you got in the ring with a coach in each corner and one in the middle, and you had to keep moving between each coach, throwing the combos they told you to. It was fast and furious. They were shouting at me to go quicker and harder. There was no rest and no bell, I just keep going and going as long as I could.

I went for what felt like ages. I was sweating buckets, my arms were heavy and my mind became foggy. I had given it 110 per cent by the time they told me that I was finished. I was physically at my end. I could do no more. My heart was beating so hard I could feel it in my neck. I couldn't breathe, and I felt I needed to keep swallowing. I started to get a pain in my back on the right side. I went into the other room and lay on the cold floor. For a moment I thought I was having a heart attack, but that feeling passed.

After a while I felt content that I knew where my physical limit was. Now it was time to taper off and

NEW YEAR, NEW ME!

rest until the big fight night. After the session was over, I was told who I would be fighting: it was a lad from the Isle of Wight. He had had a few fights before, and was quite handy by all accounts. I did my usual thing of obsessively researching. I found him on Facebook and a few of his fight videos on his boxing gym's Facebook page and studied them. There was nothing left to do; I had trained hard, I had studied the 'sweet science' of boxing. I had read book after book by boxers such as Tyson Fury, Lennox Lewis, Mike Tyson, Ricky Hatton and Carl Froch. There were a few sessions left to keep loose before fight night and then it would be my turn to 'dance under the lights'.

On the day of the fight I was a bit of a nervous wreck. I was putting loads of pressure on myself to perform. I wanted to win. I could have done with being alone and just chilling out for the day, maybe listening to some music and going for a walk. The problem was that to fight on the show, you had to sell tickets. My friends and family who brought the tickets then kept messaging me, wanting to know the plan. Then they would want to know what time I was fighting, and then they wanted to know if there was food at the venue – loads and loads of questions that I could have done without. Work Dave forgot his ticket and I had to get one of my best mates who ran the doors to get him in (thanks Scott). It was a bloody faff. It was extra stress on an already stressful day. I got to the venue early and wished I hadn't because it was just a lot of waiting around.

I talked to the other guys from the gym who were fighting, and you could cut the tension with a knife. I could see in the eyes of some of the other first-timers the same fear I was feeling. This fear made me jittery and on edge. The room was just full of the boxers and staff; no guests would be let in for at least another hour. Every boxer had to have a medical first. The medic looked exactly like the barman from *Friday Night Dinner*. People said it was actually him. I wasn't sure, and frankly not that bothered as I was crapping my pants.

I was a few weeks short of my 35th birthday and I was just about to have a scrap in front of 200-plus people. Mr Friday Night Dinner took my pulse and blood pressure, and I was asked if I was scared. Puzzled, I said yes. The medic said that was probably why I had high blood pressure, but my pulse was low. They asked me a few more questions about blood pressure and past operations, and then they gave me a clean bill of health to fight.

After all the fighters had had their medicals, the doors opened, and the venue filled up pretty quickly. The place seemed packed; people were drinking and enjoying themselves. I was picking up that the vibe of the venue had now changed: it seemed more intimidating. I was right, the vibe had changed – but it was me that felt the intimidation; everyone else was having fun. My guests arrived and settled in with drinks and food. I greeted them and sat with them for a while. I tried to focus on the early fights that were taking place but couldn't with all the people around and my guests wanting to chat.

I didn't want to seem rude, so I went backstage with the rest of the fighters from my gym and helped them prepare. I popped back to my guests every now and then to see how they were. While out back with the other lads, I felt my heart beating in my throat again. It was such a strange feeling. I thought the pressure had got to me, so I went and sat on a bench by myself to get my head in gear. I got the nod from one of the coaches that my fight was two fights away and I began to warm up. We got on the pads and the punches were flowing and I started to feel better. My body was becoming less tense, and I seemed to be relaxing. That's the power of movement.

I remember making my way to the stage and the announcer calling the name of my opponent and hearing his ring-walk music, although I can't remember what it was. Then my name was called, and my ring-walk music kicked in. I had chosen a rock song called 'Devil Inside Me' by Frank Carter & The

Rattlesnakes. I picked this song because I love it. The vast majority of the ring-walk tracks that night were of the hip hop or rap genre. Terry the coach was going to be my corner man, and he whispered, 'Take your time, don't go fast.'

I started to walk out slowly, trying not to let all the eyes get to me. I tried to look calm and collected, like this was the most normal thing in the world to me. Stepping through the ropes was like entering a new world. There wasn't anyone or anything outside of that ring. The only things that existed were me, my opponent and a referee. It's so strange how suddenly that nervousness and worry was gone, this was the only moment. The referee said some words and we trotted back to our corners, the bell went, and it was on. We both ran to the centre, touched gloves and went to war.

I wish I could tell you blow-by-blow how the fight went, but I can't. I know it happened, but I couldn't tell you how it happened. No, it's not because I got knocked out, I just don't remember. I guess it's like when a woman has a baby, they quickly forget the pain, as the myth goes. All I can remember is feeling like it was only me and him and nothing else and then the three rounds were up. I felt okay, I wasn't hurt. I had no marks. However, I had now stepped out of our little world and back into reality. I could see everyone; I could hear them with such clarity. The nervousness took over again; I wanted to get out of the ring now. I kept repeating in my head: 'Hurry up, why are they taking so long?' The referee called us into the centre of the ring, he took our hands and announced that there was a split decision.

Before I could register what he was saying he had lifted my opponent's hand. I had lost and a wave of disappointment crashed over me. I just wanted to get out of the ring and away from all the eyes. I congratulated the winner and left the ring feeling like a sorry loser. I went outside where the last remaining fighters were warming up and sat there alone to cool down. After a while one of the other coaches came up and consoled me. I sat for a while and then decided I had to put a brave face on it. I got dressed and went out to see my guests.

My best mate Rob from Stoke ran up to me and hugged me and then Charlotte came up and hugged me. They were all saying how well I had done and that I hadn't lost. Over at the bar I spied the guy that I just fought with and was in two minds about whether I should or shouldn't go over. I went over, and we got talking. Turns out he was a really nice guy. He'd had a few more fights than me and had a reputation for being a good boxer. This made me feel slightly better about losing, but not by much.

After all the fights had finished and multiple pints and shots had been bought for me by everyone, me, Si, Rob and some of my work friends moved on to a club. I was sinking the drinks down to get away from feeling like a loser. I got absolutely plastered. Si and Rob had to get me back home in a taxi where I passed out. In the morning the hangxiety mixed with the loss wasn't too pleasant and I wallowed in bed for hours. It wasn't a good idea to get drunk straight after a fight. Handling a loss while ingesting a depressant and nursing a hangover is enough to send anyone mad.

It took me two days to get over the hangover: now I am getting older it takes three. I really thought about leaving boxing at that point, but I got a call from Lee to see how I was. We chatted for 30 minutes, and he made me feel so much better. He told me about his losses and how he handled them. His words lit a fire under my arse, and two days later I was back in the gym training again.

There is a full video of my fight that has made the rounds between my friends, work friends and the guys in the gym. People have said that I have to watch it, and I will see that I wasn't as bad as I think and that the call could have gone my way. Like the old me who couldn't bring himself to look in the mirror or watch himself on home movies, the new me can't watch that video.

Chapter 12

On your Bike

BOXING ASIDE, during the training for my first fight I also completed the duathlon that I had booked, and I hadn't even trained in a block format where you run and then ride your bike straight afterwards. The closest I had got was riding a static bike in the gym and then running home. I had also been for a few long rides at the weekend through the hills of the South Downs, but done no structured triathlon-type training. I really enjoyed riding and found that after a long ride I would be in much less pain than after my long runs.

The day of the duathlon came around and I vowed that I would just go out and enjoy it. We started with a 5km run. Coach Dave's advice on this one was, 'Don't go full pelt, save your energy for the last run.' In age-old tradition I didn't listen and went full pelt from the start. I finished the 5km in good time and was happy to be in the front pack with the guys in full tri suits. I got on the bike and went full pelt again for 20km.

My 'full pelt' on a bike is much slower than everyone else's and I was overtaken a lot. The ride was 10km out and 10km back. The return 10km was difficult – the headwind was strong enough for people to stop and push their bikes. I happily ploughed on through the wind and made up a few places that I had lost.

As I got to transition, there were two entrances to the transition area, one left and one right. My belongings were on the right side and at the same time as I arrived, another person was going down the left side. They removed their helmet before going into the transition area. I did the exact same as they did in the exact same spot. This person high-fived the marshal and they ran on without issue. That same marshal then jumped over a barrier and physically grabbed my arm. He shouted at me to go back out of the area and put my helmet on and then come back in. I politely asked why, and he said, 'It's the rules, everyone must enter with their helmet on.' I pointed out that he had just high-fived a bloke with no helmet on and let him run on. He actually replied in an angry manner, 'I'm not asking him, am I?' This instantly got my back up and I asked him who the f**k he was talking to. As soon as I matched his tone, he seemed to change his tune and told me to carry on.

The muppet had cost me a good few seconds of arsing about. I racked my bike and started to run out of transition, but my legs were like jelly. I was running like a baby giraffe. I couldn't quite gauge where my step would fall. Coach Dave warned me about this, but I didn't think too much of it. I should have listened to his advice and saved my energy for the last run and spun my legs on the bike before I ran. I ran the last 7.5km and finished somewhere in the midpack. I really enjoyed it, especially the cycling. It was something different from just running.

I did try and get my running mojo back while boxing, as it's an integral part of the training. So I decided to do my own personal challenge of running my favourite route from Cocking in the South Downs to Queen Elizabeth Country Park. The South Downs challenge I comprehensively failed. It was January and we had had some heavy rain. I thought I would be fine as I had run there in the rain before, although never at this time of year. Charlotte dropped me off around 8am and asked if I really wanted to do this. It was grey and dark with a chilly breeze. I told her I would be fine, and I would call when I was close to the park for her to pick me up.

I got out of the nice warm car and immediately felt that breeze cut through my running top. I wished I had brought a windbreaker. Charlotte drove off, leaving me wishing I had stayed in bed and was not about to run up a massive hill. This hill wasn't too bad; it was mainly hard compact dirt and rock, but when I got to the top, it was a different story. The path at the top of the hill disappeared into what can only be described as a brown lake. There was no way I was going to ring Charlotte to turn around and come get me, so I went through it.

The water went over my ankles, and the bottom was mud that was threatening to suck me into the centre of the earth. My feet and trainers were soaking wet. I carried on. The paths were much the same: massive puddles of thick, sticky mud. I forgot about getting a PB on this course – my new goal was to stay alive and not fall over. The going was so slow that I got cold and started to shiver a lot. I could no longer feel my feet. I kept repeating to myself, THIS WAS A BAD IDEA.

The worst was yet to come. I got to a part of the route that was a steep grass hill. This hill is basically impossible to run up even in the summer due to its steepness. This time I couldn't even walk up it. I would get a few steps up and slip even further back. I had to get on my hands and knees and crawl up. I wasn't even halfway yet. I was soaking wet, shivering, and now with dirty knees and hands. There was no clear running. It was all stop and start. I was getting too cold and tried to ring Charlotte, but she didn't answer, so I trudged on.

I felt so miserable, I just wanted to stop. I slid down a hill, and now my arse, running pack, and the back of my head were covered in mud. I checked my watch and had only 10km to go. I tried Charlotte again, and this time she answered. I told her what was going on. I asked her to meet me at the end and bring a flask of tea, a towel and a warm jumper. I managed to get to the country park, where I saw the first people I had seen for the last four hours. I was getting funny looks, number one because I looked like I was some sort of swamp monster, and number two, who in their right mind would do that route in this weather at this time of the year?

Charlotte was waiting for me. I wasn't allowed to get in the car in the state I was in, so I had to take my shoes and socks off. My feet were blue and had no feeling whatsoever. They really worried me. I had to take my top off to put the jumper on and wear the towel as a skirt. I got in and drank a scalding hot flask of tea. I shivered for the full 20 minutes on the way home despite the car blowers being on full blast. It took me a couple of days to feel normal again. I said to Charlotte and the kids, 'No more running.' They didn't believe me, but I was really fed up with it for some reason. I decided to concentrate on the boxing.

With my running mojo well and truly gone, I was enjoying my fight preparation and cycling. I thought it would be a good idea to do a 100km cycling race in the New Forest. The training to get to 100km was harder than I imagined. Also, I naively thought that the New Forest was flat. I had to chuck in some hard hill training while I learned the craft of cycling. I had some near-misses with other road users. I have never been an angry road user. I am normally quite placid. However, some of the muppets on the road made me furious.

One woman felt the full force of my rage while I was cycling up a rather steep hill leading to Petersfield. She tried to pass me going up a very steep section, but was far too close, and couldn't see over the crest. Inevitably, a car came the other way. She had no option other than turning her car into me, pinning me into a bush. Her car was physically touching me. I began to thump the car as hard as I could to get her off of me. Rather than moving to let me out of the bush she stopped. She then began to shout at me as if I was in the wrong. I told her to move her car so I could get out of the bush and call the police as she had hit me with her car.

The car that had come over the hill had also stopped. They were telling her to move and let me out. She then turned her attention to the other driver and unleashed a barrage of foul language towards them. I took the opportunity to try and move her car using my pedal. Unfortunately, all it did was leave a massive gouge down to the metal up her passenger door. She eventually drove off, wheels spinning at speed, no doubt to go and try to kill another cyclist. That experience left me fuming for days.

Another time, two blokes in a white van coming towards me threw a grape that hit me in the chest. It really hurt. If it had hit me in my face, it could have caused some real damage. I cycled after them. I managed to catch them at a set of traffic lights, and I punched their passenger wing mirror completely off. Both the men looked panicked as I tried to open the door while screaming profanities at them. The light went green, and they drove off. As I recovered my composure and cooled down, I realised I was outside a hairdressers, and a bunch of older ladies were gawking at me. I cut my ride short and went home. Now while driving I always ensure I give cyclists as much room as possible because I know what they go through.

I continued dual training. I was mixing long bike rides with boxing sessions. It felt good to mix things up. Apart from the odd muppet driver, training was going well. The 100km ride came around quickly and I felt ready for it. I had done 80km in training, so adding 20km to make it 100km would surely be doable. I treated myself to a fancy Garmin bike computer so I could load up the GPS route. I didn't want to get lost in the New Forest. I invested in some spare inner tubes and a fancy CO_2 pump. I had my food and drink, and I was ready to go.

I made my way to the event. I was surprised at how busy it was and how many different bikes I could see. There were some expensive machines out for this ride, some of them worth more than my car. I made my way to the start line. It felt different from a running event. People seemed to mix more and chat at a running event, but this seemed more like little groups of friends everywhere. There weren't many single riders. Never mind, I would stick my headphones on and go for it. I also noticed that rather than everyone starting at once or in waves, the start line seemed to be open, and you went when you were ready.

I checked my kit and went. In the first few kilometres, there was a big sign saying 'Sand on the road'. The sand was at the bottom of a rather steep hill close to a beach area. I could see a group of people and bikes around someone on the floor. I couldn't quite see, but it seemed like they had come off and scraped their face along the floor. Nasty! I would have to pay way more attention in a cycling event. The speeds I would be doing could cause some real damage.

The first 30km were easy, riding through some lovely forest and open headland areas. At the first big feed station, I filled up my bottles and started to chat to one of the marshals who warned me the next section was hilly. Then all of a sudden, we heard a loud screeching and a load of shouting. A Land Rover had attempted to overtake a group of cyclists turning into the feed station – yet another reminder that cycling can be dangerous.

I set off for the hills and I can tell you there were a couple of hard climbs which didn't provide me with much trouble. By no means was I Lance Armstrong – the Lycra whippets left me in their dust – but I felt good and strong. The route took us through the famous village of Beaulieu. At the same time, there must have been a classic car show on in the area. I was drooling while riding past some pristine Jaguars and Morgans. Leaving Beaulieu, I came across the famous New Forest ponies that wander freely. There was a group of them just standing in the road, blocking both sides. The cars just sat there waiting as I tentatively manoeuvred past them and the ponies.

I only started to feel fatigued around the 70km mark. I stopped at the next feed station and got off the bike. My legs felt wobbly, and my arse had begun to hurt. I filled up my bottles and went on my way, thinking that I didn't plan to stop again. Only 10km later my arse had deteriorated. The hard seat and bumpy road were giving it a pounding. I tried to stand up on my pedals as much as possible, but when I did, my calves hurt. At 80km my arse was in big trouble. The pain was shooting up that little bit between your man parts and your bum.

I kept going, but with only 10km left, I had to stop and have a little stand up. After a couple of minutes' rest, I did the last 10km and thankfully crossed the finish line, arse in one piece. I did it in 4hr 25min. I collected my medal, threw my bike in the car and tentatively lowered my arse into the car and sat for a good while before attempting to drive home along the M27.

Chapter 13

A Shot at Redemption!

GOING BACK into the gym after I had lost my fight was hard to start with. I had this strange notion that people would laugh or be disappointed in me for losing. That first time back I was purposefully late. I wanted to miss the part where everyone stands waiting in the corridor chatting while the kids finish their session. I sat in the car, not wanting to get out. I had to force myself to walk back through them gym doors. Unsurprisingly, I was greeted as normal. These were good people, so why would I think they would laugh at me? I got some pats on the back and a few fist bumps. As the session went on, I became more relaxed and felt I could be open about losing. I started to talk to the others about the loss and feeling shit about it. This was a weight off my shoulders as the other guys started to share stories about fights they had lost.

I quickly realised that the majority of the people in the gym had lost at least once in their career. I tried to think of it as similar to when I had played rugby. I lost many games but never once felt crap about it. That's because in a team sport, a loss doesn't seem as bad because you share the disappointment and guilt across many shoulders. In boxing, a loss is only on your shoulders, but this was white-collar boxing: you win some, you lose some, no one's a pro. It's meant to be fun and to get you fit.

Even though I had this new attitude, I decided I wasn't going to lose again, so I stepped up my training. People asked how I could step up my training more than I was doing – well, I started to wake up an hour earlier and go to the gym, do a full-strength workout and then go to work. After work, I would either be in the boxing gym or out for a run. Sunday would be the only rest day I had, but I wouldn't really rest. I would end up going for long walks with the dogs and jogging with them for a little while. Every single night I would do yoga. This was my workout schedule.

Day	AM	PM	Night
Monday	1 hour strength training	Run at least 6km	Yoga
Tuesday	1 hour strength training	Boxing	Yoga
Wednesday	1 hour strength training	Run at least 6km	Yoga
Thursday	1 hour strength training	Boxing	Yoga
Friday	1 hour strength training	Run at least 6km	Yoga
Saturday	Boxing	Long run	Yoga
Sunday	Walking	Rest	Yoga

I did this week in, week out. I dropped some more weight, but my arms and shoulders started to look ripped. I had never had this before and I looked good. I certainly felt more confident in social and work situations, and I saw that what I was doing was having a positive effect on my wife and kids. They were proud of me, we went out more and my relationship with my wife got better.

However, I didn't feel physically good. My dizzy spells started to get worse. One time after a long run, I was in the garden cooling down at the table. When I stood up, a fuzzy darkness from the edge of my vision started to close in around me, and I could hear a strange, tinny, whooping sound in my ears.

The funny thing is that these episodes felt nice; the fuzzy, tingly feeling in my body felt good, and the dizzy, spacey feeling made me feel high. I tried to ignore it and put it down to needing more food as my blood sugars were low. I started to get this flu-like heaviness in my body every morning. I felt like I was in a battle against gravity, and it was winning. This became the new normal. My sleep became deep and dreamless. It felt almost like when you are drunk, and you pass out rather than go to sleep.

After a while, I had to stop my Saturday long run and Sunday walk. To replace them, I would stay in bed for half of the day and then spend the rest dozing on the sofa. I was still unusually susceptible to the cold, or as my nan would say, I was 'nesh'. I was always in a hoodie or covered up with a blanket. Summer rolled around, and any breeze or cold water caused me to shiver like a leaf. We went camping again in Dorset as a family, with Si and Rob's families. I suffered really badly at night. I would have to wear multiple layers of clothes. We took the paddleboards to a lake surrounded by hills; the sun was blazing and the kids were loving it. I couldn't bring myself to get into the water, because I knew I would shiver. I avoided anything that I thought would make me cold, and I started to travel everywhere with a jumper. The only time I wasn't cold to my core was when I was training or running.

Despite all these weird symptoms, including numb thumbs, I kept training. I even entered a trail half marathon and ran my half marathon PB. I knew training at this level couldn't last and at some point, I would injure myself. On one of my non-boxing days, I was out running along the shore at Langstone Harbour. When the tide is out, it uncovers a rocky and sea-weedy path that you can run along from Hayling Island to Emsworth. It was late afternoon, and I was running quickly, too quickly considering I had only just started and hadn't warmed up. I was running on a particularly slimy and weedy section with the path hidden underneath.

My heel came down hard on a hidden rock wrapped in slime. My foot slipped straight off and folded underneath me. A laser-like shooting pain went straight up the outside of my leg and into my knee. As that pain shot up my leg, I began to fall sideways in what felt like slow motion. I couldn't get my folded foot from under me quickly enough to stop the inevitable. I hit the deck hard! I had tried to put my hand out to stop myself but as the rocks were slimy and wet my hand slipped straight off, and I hit the jagged rocks with full force on my right side. Out of sheer embarrassment, I shot up off the floor and quickly looked around to see if some lucky person had witnessed me hitting the deck and was now crying with laughter. Thank the universe, no one saw me, and I stopped pretending I wasn't hurt. I slowly limped to the sea wall and lay down, while mentally checking my injuries. Ankle? Knackered. Hip? Aching. Ribs? Bruised. Hands? Slimy. Dignity? Gone.

I dragged myself off that wall and limped home. In the morning, I was pretty much okay other than my ankle, which was swollen and bruised. No way was I going to the gym. I couldn't even put any weight on my right leg without pains shooting up it. I had to take my laces out of my work shoes to get them on. It was a nightmare. I had training to do. I needed to be in that boxing gym. I couldn't afford to take any enforced time off.

Unfortunately, I had to take just over two weeks off and rest my ankle. This did my body good but not my mind. I was constantly concerned that I was missing valuable training time. My worry began to manifest itself mainly as irritability. I became aggressive and snappy at Charlotte and the kids. When they tried to talk to me, I genuinely wanted them to stop and leave me alone. It began to affect my sleep, and I realised that I was suffering with anxiety. Then I ended up berating myself for feeling this way, and when I did this, I felt worse.

This anxiety stayed with me while I slowly got back to training. My assumption as to why I was still experiencing anxiety changed from not being able to train to being scared of losing my next fight. I remember having to apologise to Charlotte for snapping at her for something stupid like the TV being on too loud. (I swear my kids and wife are deaf. The TV is always so loud.) I told her it was because I was worried about the upcoming fight.

If I am honest, it wasn't just the fight; I was still having the dizzy spells. I had periods of time where I couldn't concentrate at work. I would look at a spreadsheet and not understand anything I was seeing. People would be talking to me, and I would zone out. I did the worst thing you can do in these situations, and I consulted Dr Google. I put all my symptoms in to the search bar, including my numb thumbs and always being cold. Can you guess what came back? Mainly the big C and things like brain-eating parasites. I thought, 'Shit, what if I do have something like that?' I made a deal with myself to go to the doctor after the fight. Very stupid of me, I know – I should have gone to see an expert straight away. What I chose to do instead was box and also run a trail half marathon near Queen Elizabeth Country Park. The race went well, and I spent some of the time with the skinny-vest crew near the front pack before fading away mid-run. I finished somewhere in the mid-pack and was happy that I had done well even though I wasn't prioritising running at the time.

The worst of my dizzy symptoms came at the peak of my training block before starting to taper before the fight. I was in the smaller room of the gym, where we were doing the classic 'shark tank'. My first and second rounds went well. In my third, I started to feel strange. My arms and feet became tingly. I felt this sudden, strange tickling sensation in my chest. I felt as though something was lightly stroking my heart with a feather. I backed off from the fight. Out the corner of my eye, I saw that there were only 30 seconds left, so I tucked up and defended myself.

The time was up, and I stepped through the ropes. I was standing on the edge of the ring, one hand on the ropes and one on the corner pads. I was panicking, thinking that I was having a heart attack, then my vision started to go. Again, darkness started from the outside of my eye and worked its way into the centre. My hearing became muffled, as if a quilt had been placed over my head. My legs went weak, and I knew I was going to faint. I fell backwards.

Luckily, I was standing on a bit of the ring with a wall behind me. I hit the wall with my back and the back of my head. The movement of me hitting the wall caused a shock that brought me back around. My vision and hearing came back in an instant. The tickling in my chest had gone. I then noticed everyone looking at me. My face flushed with blood, I felt embarrassed, and I managed to quietly say I had slipped off the ring. Everyone seemed to buy what I said, and they got on with what they were all doing.

It was close to the end of the session, so I made my excuses and left early. I was worried, but still, I didn't go to seek professional help. All sorts of things were going through my head. I was telling myself I was working too hard and suffering from stress. I told myself I was putting too much pressure on myself to train and I certainly didn't want to lose my fight. Looking back, it's crazy what I was putting myself through and never even mentioned to the people I love: I kept it all inside.

A SHOT AT REDEMPTION!

It even started to manifest at work. One of the guys at work was retiring. Work Dave, my boss Charlotte and I went out for lunch with Brian. We were sitting in the restaurant eating and chatting away. All of a sudden, I started to sweat profusely for no reason. My work shirt went see-through, and I had to excuse myself and go outside. I was confused by what was happening. I was normally cold, and now here I was feeling as if I was on fire. It wasn't just the top half of my body. My legs were dripping. I had never felt anything like it. I was sweating as if I had just finished a full training session in the desert. Everyone I was with was concerned and suggested I go and get checked out. I wish I had listened. Instead, I went back to the office and sat in front of two fans. I must have stunk for the rest of the day.

The next session in the boxing gym was a light one as we were getting close to fight night. As soon as I started to punch, I experienced deep aching in my forearms. The pain was so bad I had to stop and go home. It was two weeks to the fight, and in those two weeks I did nothing, no training and no punching. I didn't lift a finger. I lay on the sofa and read books and watched crap on the TV. I wanted all my symptoms to stop before the fight, and I felt it was best to rest and recover with a hope that on fight night I would be itching to box.

Fight night was upon us, and my two weeks' rest did nothing, as I was dreading it. At times I was shaking just thinking about getting in the ring. I couldn't pull out because people would think that I was weak or scared. I was wishing for all sorts of things to happen so that the event would be called off – bomb scare, tidal wave, any of those things would have done. A black swan event wasn't to happen though, so I had to attend and fight.

It was a standard procedure, pain in the arse trying to organise my guests, the text messages and phone calls non-stop. It was like herding cats. I got to the venue early with the other fighters for my medical. Again, I was told my heart rate was low, but blood pressure was high: the medics signed me off anyway. I put my bag under the table where my guests would be sitting, and I left the venue. I lay on the beach for a while trying to relax. Normally I would have put my headphones on and stuck on some high-tempo music to get me pumped up and ready to fight, but I didn't. I put on some lo-fi hip-hop beats and tried to chill the anxiety and dread out of me. This obviously didn't work, and it was getting to the time that the venue would start letting guests in.

I made my way back past the queues of people waiting outside. Mine was due to be the last fight of the night, which meant that my guests would be coming a little later than before. I was on my own for a while and watched a few of the kids' fights first. When my people started to show up, I was wishing I could be alone again. I was asked multiple questions about being the last fight of the night. They were all talking as if it was the main event. This increased the pressure I was putting on myself and I felt physically sick.

I tried to explain that I didn't think it worked like that in white-collar boxing, but it didn't stop them. There were a lot of fights being crammed in on this card, and my fight was due at 10.30pm. This means I was knocking about in the venue from 6.30pm. That was four hours of worry and stress. If I felt this bad waiting to fight in front of a couple of hundred people, then God knows what the professionals like Tyson Fury and Oleksandr Usyk go through. At around 9pm, I went backstage and stayed there until it was my time to fight.

A few of the other fights overran, so it wasn't until after 10pm that I started to warm up on the pads. Strangely, as soon as I began to move and punch, move and punch, I started to feel better and began to relax. The rhythmic pop, pop, pop of my glove hitting the bags was soothing. It really is a satisfying feeling when you snap your punches to get a nice pop on impact. To me it's one of the best feelings in the world. I was warm, my blood was flowing, and I was now ready to get it over with. It was time to fight.

I took my shirt off, my hands were wrapped, and my gum shield was in. There was nothing else to do – it was time to punch and be punched. My opponent was called first, and I saw him walk out from the other side of the stage. He looked cool and calm. He looked like a killer. This was the opposite of what I felt. Surely inside he felt worried like me? I put my game face on. I wanted to look like him, like a killer. I wanted the coaches, guests and venue staff to think this was just another fight for me, no big deal. This is what I do, I'm not scared.

I waited a couple of seconds for my music to kick in. I took several big breaths in through my nose and I walked out. Surprise hit me square in the jaw, half the place was empty. Where had everyone gone? While I was out back worrying myself to death, people had been watching their loved ones and mates fight and then left to celebrate in the pubs and clubs of Portsmouth. It was now almost 11pm after all. I felt a small release of pressure that allowed me to puff out my chest a little more. I looked around at the faces that were left in the venue as they screamed and shouted for blood. As soon as I stepped through the ropes, the same thing happened as the first time. The screaming people outside of the ring no longer existed. It was me, him, and the referee – there was no one else in our little world.

We got the referee's rules and touched gloves. I went back to my corner and felt ready to go. *Ding ding*. I ran into the middle immediately, throwing out two straight jabs. In return, a right-hand haymaker came my way, but it missed. It went on like this for three rounds. He snapped my head back a couple of times, and I snapped his. I tried to throw a few uppercuts, only really landing one, but we were both quite defensive fighters and preferred to pick our punches rather than go all-guns-blazing.

In the ring I felt good. I felt comfortable and loose, and the previous dread, fear and anxiety had melted away. The bell went to signify the end. We had a sweaty man-hug and congratulated each other. We went to our corners. As my corner man was pulling off my gloves, he was telling me I had this in the bag. I felt confident that I had won. In that ring, it's hard to tell who has the upper hand. For me, it's hard to remember much from what happened in that ring. I have talked to lads about fights I have watched them in, talking blow by blow what they did. I end up thinking, 'What fight were you in? Because it's not the one I watched.' I can't see how they remember.

The referee called us into the middle and took our hands. The announcer was on the mic giving it loads of chat, thanking everyone for coming and all that rubbish. My opponent and I shared a look of bemusement, both thinking the same thing. Get on with it, we haven't got all night. The moment came. For me time slowed down, every second slowed to a minute. I was looking at the floor. The verdict was announced, and it was a draw. Both of our hands were raised.

We had a hug in the ring and a chat. He seemed to be a good guy, and I was happy to share a ring with him. It's a strange feeling that before a fight you plan to take this person's head clean off. Then you get in a ring, and you knock ten tons of crap out of each other. After you have fought, you are mates – both of you have shared an experience that hardly anyone else will. We had a quick drink together, and I noticed a few marks on his face and had a little smile to myself. It's a funny situation. I have seen this guy lots of times since that fight, and we always shake hands and have a chat. He even messaged me the other day looking for a job as one of his friends works for me. I would happily give him a job if I had one.

We got out of the ring and the event organisers started to take apart the ring straight away. I didn't go out back to get my stuff. I went straight over to my guests for a chat and then got a few beers with them. As we were the last fight, more people started to leave.

My friends and workmates were trying to get me to go out clubbing. I flat-out refused as I didn't want to be in the same place as after my last fight – I didn't want to spend the next day feeling sorry for myself. I put on my jacket and left with Charlotte and two of our friends.

To celebrate my draw, we went to a Portsmouth institution on top of Portsdown Hill, Mick's Monster Burgers. If you haven't been there, you must. The burger van overlooks the whole of Portsmouth. From its vantage point, you can see the Isle of Wight and miles out to sea. They sell massive burgers and some of the best cheesy chips I have ever had (this isn't an ad, by the way). We ate our food; I treated myself to a Monster Burger, which contained enough meat to feed a family of four. Overlooking the twinkling island city lights of Portsmouth, watching slow-moving ships sail across the black sea, I felt content and happy.

We had a good chat on that hill, and I decided I wasn't going to box again. It wasn't the fact that I hadn't been successful. After all, I had only had two fights. It was that I no longer wanted to experience the anxiety and dread I had felt before the bouts. We went home and I slept soundly, safe in the knowledge that I had given it a good go.

The next morning, I was up early and feeling as fresh as a daisy, with no hangover. I had developed a nice black eye in the night and a few glove scuffs, but that was fine. I got my bike out of the garage and pedalled my way up the hills of the South Downs. It was a perfect autumn day, it wasn't too cold, and the sky was clear. I felt free from stress and worry, and that just confirmed to me that my anxiety had been caused by the boxing and the pressure I had put on myself to win. I knew I was best off not fighting again.

I stopped on a hill not far from a little church in the middle of nowhere called St Hubert's. As I sat under a tree looking across the hills, I had a moment and really reflected on where I had come from: a 24-stone mess of a man that couldn't look at himself in the mirror or in photos, to running marathons and ultra marathons; to having the balls to take off my shirt and fight other men in front of a baying, drunk crowd. I felt a sense of pride. I had done well and now it was time to move on. It was time to go back to running. I sat there making plans to hit my goal of running for 24 hours, and then I wanted to sort my swimming out and smash a triathlon. This was now my focus. I rode home a happy man to start my planning and preparation. Little did I know at the time that a massive kick in the crotch would derail my new plans.

Chapter 14
Back to Running

ALTHOUGH I had made the decision not to fight again, I didn't want to close the door on it completely. I thought I might want to go back at some point, so I told the lads in the gym that I was going to do a couple of running challenges and then come back to boxing. I thought, 'You never know Kyle, you could actually miss all the stress and anxiety.' I could be one of those special people who thrive on it. Making the decision alleviated a lot of the stress I was feeling, and my strange symptoms had faded slightly, but I was still freezing cold all the time and dizzy now and then.

I decided not to go to the doctor to be told I was suffering from stress and anxiety. I thought I was weak for not being able to handle it. In the weeks following the fight I only cycled and ran a few 5kms. It was low-intensity stuff that kept me ticking over. I started to plan my event calendar. I really enjoy sitting on the sofa and researching and planning events. I then loved to watch YouTube videos of events. It sounds sad, I know, but it's my favourite thing to do.

I found a 24-hour race in London for the following year. The event consisted of a 5km loop. You could either choose to do it on your own until you dropped or you could enter as a team and do it relay-style. I was going to do it alone and stuck it in my calendar. I planned to do the Run to the Sea Brighton 50km again as a training run for my 24-hour race; I wanted to beat my original time. I also planned to do the Clarendon Marathon again, the one which I had badly failed. The next year was looking to be a busy time for running events and I was super excited to get out there and be doing what I did best.

I had all the plans for next year set and now I wondered what I should do to finish off 2022. There weren't that many events locally going on, so I booked up the RNLI 10km in December and a duathlon. I wanted to beat my previous duathlon time and get a 10km PB. I set about training. The duathlon was up first, so I did blocks of run, cycle, run and could manage the distance easily enough but my speed was off, and I found it difficult to get close to the times I had been doing before I stopped boxing. I felt that something wasn't right: maybe the ankle injury during my second fight and not running as much had caused a decline in my pace and endurance. I became tired more quickly than usual when I tried to hold pace for a long time.

I kept at it and trained in line with Coach Dave's suggestions. I had just started to feel comfortable with pace again when the duathlon came around. On the day when I turned up to the start with all my gear, I had a flashback to the marshal from my last duathlon, the one I nearly punched. I hoped that I wouldn't recognise him or, even worse, him recognise me. I started the run and was more patient than I had been in my first event, I didn't go hell for leather. I stayed with the mid-pack and planned to make up places on the bike.

I ran into transition and got my bike kit on smoothly, remembering to helmet up first. On the cycling leg I remained patient as in the first run and stayed with the mid-pack. To be fair I didn't have a choice as the Lycra-clad brigade were way too fast for me, but I did admire their sunglasses and tri bars as they shot past me. I wished I could pull off those sporty cycling glasses but my head's too big: they look funny on me. This time before transition I remembered to drop the gears I was in and spin my legs (thank you Coach Dave). The idea is to get some feeling in your legs so you are not running like a baby giraffe when you get off the bike.

I didn't take my helmet off early and didn't see the marshal that had had a pop at me last time, lucky for him. I then got on to my second run and my legs weren't as jellified as the first duathlon and I tried to put the pace on but found I couldn't. I was just too tired. My breathing was good, but I couldn't push any more energy out. I stayed with the mid-pack and finished the race without putting much pace on. I didn't beat my first duathlon time despite being fitter and more muscular than during the first one. I wasn't disappointed at all – I got a nice medal and I was just getting back into this stuff properly after my illustrious boxing career.

After the duathlon, I put my bike away for the winter and concentrated solely on running. I had the RNLI 10km coming up, and I wanted to do it with pace and get a personal best. I looked at the course, and it was a completely flat two 5km laps on Southsea Common. There would be no roads, cars or bikes to contend with. There would only be a few dog walkers, and the horrible winter weather could get in the way. It was the perfect course for a PB. I got cracking with lots of interval sessions. I wanted to see if I was able to get my pace back up in under a month and a half.

After a couple of weeks, I felt it was coming back, and Coach Dave kept increasing the pace I needed to hold for each interval. During one of these hard interval sessions, I had a funny turn. It was around 6pm. I had got home from work and grabbed a quick snack as usual. I spent the requisite amount of time talking to Charlotte about her day before getting my running gear on and hitting the road. I remember it was pouring down with rain, and I knew it would be cold.

To stave off the chill, I had begun to wear two pairs of socks and a pair of thin running gloves with a pair of woollen gloves over the top. I knew when I got home, I would have to ask Charlotte to feel the temperature of the shower or bath water because my hands would be too numb to. I would not be able to tell if the water was freezing or scalding hot. I went out into the cold, rainy night. In the summer I longed for rain to cool me down, but now I could think of nothing worse. I started with a few km warm-up, and it was nice and easy. My Garmin watch informed me that I had completed my warm-up, and next would be my first interval. I got through three or four when I started to feel my heart in my throat, and I started to gasp for air like a fish out of water.

This stopped me in my tracks. I couldn't run. I didn't know what was going on. It felt like an alien was going to pop right out of my neck and upper chest. I got my phone out, about to call for help. But I am one of those silly men that doesn't like to ask for help, so I kept telling myself to get home and you'll be okay, just get home and it will be fine. After a while walking back towards home, the feelings subsided, and my heart rate went back to normal. The only problem now was that I was soaking wet and shivering. I called Charlotte and asked her to run me a bath and keep an eye on the temperature. When I arrived at the door, Charlotte let me in and could tell there was something wrong. She said I looked like a ghost, not as if I had seen a ghost, but I was white as a ghost. I said I was cold and didn't feel well and all I needed was a nice warm bath and some hot food.

For the next few days, I had a sleepy, tired feeling. It wasn't that I felt exhausted but as if I just wanted to curl up in a warm bed and sleep for a few days. In some respects, it was a nice feeling, but I was struggling to stay awake at work. I was lucky I had my own office so I could close the door and rest my eyes. It came to a head when I couldn't concentrate on anything. I couldn't read a book or watch the TV. Nothing was sinking in. I tried to get an appointment at the doctor's three times over three days. While I was on hold in the queue, all the appointments had gone. On my fourth attempt, I secured an appointment. I was over the moon that I managed to get in. I felt like what I would imagine National Lottery winners feel like when they find out they have hit the jackpot. The appointment was on Thursday, and I had my RNLI 10km planned for Saturday.

I turned up at the doctor's and, unusually, went straight in to see him. I thought I would be in for a wait. I sat down and felt a weird, nervous feeling. I don't like going to the doctor's. I feel like a naughty boy having to sit across from the headmaster and explain my actions. Anyhow, he asked me how he could help and I listed off my symptoms:

- Dizzy
- Tired
- Can't concentrate
- Always cold
- Memory is rubbish
- Heart beating in my throat
- Anxiety
- Numb thumbs

He asked me a few questions about my lifestyle: did I drink? Yes. Did I smoke? No. Did I take drugs? No. Did I exercise? Yes. I went through my whole story of being 24 stone, being told I wouldn't be able to run much by my surgeon, to running ultra marathons and boxing. He said he was impressed by my weight loss and how I had managed to turn my health around. He did some tests and then listened to my heart. I could tell there might be something wrong because the mood changed in the room slightly. The doctor had become quiet and stopped chatting.

He went over to his computer, did some typing, and then listened to my heart again. After a while, he told me that he would like me to have an ECG (electrocardiogram) as he just wanted to check my heart to be sure everything was okay. He asked me to sit in the waiting area, and I would be called through. I was stumped. What could be wrong? Heart issues are pretty heavy stuff. You can't live without a heart.

After 30 minutes of speculating about what was wrong with me, I heard my name called out. I followed the nurse into a small, dimly lit room. I thought this was definitely where pregnant women have scans. The nurse asked me to remove my top. It was a good job I had had a shower in the morning and slapped on a bit of Brut, I thought. She then asked me to roll up my trouser leg, as if it was some sort of masonic initiation. She asked me to lie on the bed, and then she began to stick patches all over my chest, side, wrist and ankle. She attached the wires, and she told me to relax all my muscles.

I didn't realise I was holding my stomach in. That's an overhanging behaviour I had from being so big. If on the odd chance I had to remove my top, I would breathe in to look less fat. The test began, and as I lay there, I now felt quite relaxed. After a few minutes, she said she just needed to let the doctor know something.

She was gone from the room for ages. I was lying there for about 15 minutes on my own. I nearly dozed off. Eventually, she came back in alone. 'That's a good sign,' I thought. She said that an appointment would be made for me to go for an echocardiogram at the local health centre. 'Bad sign,' I thought. She said they would give me a call to organise it. I asked if everything was okay and she said everything is fine, but the doctor just wants to be sure. I couldn't help but feel I was getting mixed messages.

I told Charlotte about what happened at the doctor's when I got home. She asked me when the health centre would be in touch. I flippantly said probably a few weeks. Not 20 minutes after I said that, I got a call asking me to attend the health centre at eight o'clock the next morning. Bad sign. I had a poor night's sleep and dragged myself to the health centre first thing on Friday. It was pretty quiet, and I found myself floating through dimly lit halls towards the imaging department.

Again, no waiting, I was straight through. The nurse was an older lady and not shy about telling me I was a nice, tall, handsome boy. She said it in that way older ladies do, half joking, but half given the chance they would jump you. 'Top off.' Oh, here we go, I thought. We were having a good chat while she rubbed jelly stuff on me with her wand. I was asked to turn on my side with my back to her while she reached over me, moving the wand over my chest. Reaching over caused her to push her body close to my back and I could feel her pressing against me. This was turning into a Carry On film. 'Oh, Matron,' was running through my head.

Then came the strange bit, the recording of the sound of my heart. She turned on the speaker and I could hear this strange whooshing sound. It was nothing like you would expect your heart to sound. The procedure thankfully came to an end, and I whipped the excess jelly off my chest. I could feel the nurse's greedy eyes all over my glistening body (I'm joking; she was looking at her computer). I asked if everything was okay and she said she didn't interpret the readings, but she would send them to the doctor who had ordered the test. I asked how long, and she told me that they should be in touch within two weeks.

I went off to work and tried to put it to the back of my mind. I had a race to run the next day, and I wasn't going to pull out. I had already paid my money. I told Work Dave about what was going on and he said not to do the race. If there was something wrong, it could do damage. I pretended to listen and take on board what he was saying and lied that I would think about it. Charlotte also challenged me, but when I said I was doing it, she supported me. Life insurance money?

I did well to put the tests I had to the back of my mind, and I slept like a baby. I woke on the Saturday morning excited and ready to run, until I opened the curtains and saw it was grey and drizzling outside. Great, it was going to be a cold run and the course on Southsea Common would be exposed to the wind coming off the sea. I had a few rounds of toast with peanut butter and a massive strong coffee: the fuel of champions. I did think about trying Usain Bolt's fuelling of chicken nuggets before a race, but for me that would be like waving around heroin in front of an addict.

As it was only a 10km I didn't need much gear. I just took some water, and I put my dry robe in the car for afterwards. I drove down to the race along the seafront towards the common. It was miserable; the drizzle was now coming in horizontally off the sea. There wasn't a soul out. I got to the common and it was empty. In the centre, I could see a couple of gazebos and some flags to signify a start and finish line. There were only a few people milling about. I didn't think the weather was that bad for people to not show up. I then noticed that every other car parked along the front was full. Everyone was waiting for the last possible minute to get out of the car and get to the start line. They were savouring the last few moments of warmth.

When I saw people start wandering over to the start, I joined them. There weren't that many people there for this race. I would say less than 150 – maybe the weather had put people off. Most were wearing bin bags or trying to shelter from the rain. To me, it didn't matter; in about ten minutes, we would all be wet when we started to run. There was no chatting or fun race warm-ups to start, just a man with a megaphone who called us to the start and explained the route and some of the dangers we might face. He explained that we would need to do two laps and at the end of the second, we would then make our way to the finish flags down the tunnel of barriers. He stopped talking and without saying another word, pushed the siren on the megaphone and we were off.

As soon as we started to run, I felt great. My tiredness was gone, and I felt energised. I was running in the front of the mid-pack. I could see that there were only ten or so people in front of me. I went for it. Halfway through the first lap, I decided to go all out. I avoided the muddy puddles with the grace of a gazelle. With a mixture of rain and sweat reaching my lips, I began to pick people off one by one. By the start of the second lap, I was in third place. Second wasn't that far ahead, but every time I got close, he put on some pace and got away from me. After a few attempts, I knew I wasn't going to take him unless he blew up and slowed right down, but the chances were I would be the one blowing up. There was a man on a bike leading the person in first place around the course, and when we were getting close to lapping the slow runners, he would shout to let us past. This little thing made me feel really good. I had never been in that position before. I had been the one who was lapped.

My only goal was now to hold third place until the end. This was difficult. Halfway through the second lap, my lungs were burning, and my quads were heavy. I thought I had it in me, but I didn't realise there was someone on my tail. As we rounded a corner off the grass and on to the pavement, I could hear him. I gritted my teeth and put what little pace I had left through my legs, but he was still there. I could feel him closing me down. I saw the finish line and entered the barrier tunnel. Just as I had entered, the lad overtook me. He was just playing with me all along. He had way more energy in the tank and used it for a sprint finish. I crossed the line in fourth. The second time I had come fourth in a race.

I was disappointed that I hadn't been able to hold on to third. I had to be happy as I had finished fourth by a pretty wide margin. Fifth place didn't cross the finish line until a good 30 seconds after me. I collected my medal and a small goodie bag. Nobody was waiting around because of the weather. I didn't want to wait either, so I went to the car and wrapped myself up in my dry robe. I sat there with the heaters on full blast. While I warmed up, I did a braggy Instagram post and messaged Coach Dave. He looked at my stats and congratulated me. He specifically mentioned my heart rate being great.

As I warmed up, I started to feel really uncomfortable, like there was loads of pressure in my head. It kind of felt as it does when you are bunged up with the flu. I started to feel dizzy, so I closed my eyes for a bit. When I opened them and had a look around, most of the cars that were around me had gone and my windows were steamed up. God knows how long my eyes had been closed; I don't think I fell asleep. I started to drive back home along the seafront when I had to pull over. I got out of the car, jumped down to the stony beach, and puked up. It was that yellow bile that burns your throat as it comes up. I felt terrible. When I managed to get home, I sorted myself out and got back into bed. I knew something was really wrong with me. Confirmation was about to come.

Chapter 15

It All Makes Sense Now

I SPENT the Saturday recovering in bed; I must have slept for 15 hours straight. On Sunday I just chilled on the sofa watching rubbish TV. I am no good at relaxing – I have to always be doing something, or I get bored. If I do nothing, I feel guilty. Sure enough, I got bored and did the wrong thing again and consulted Dr Google and listed my symptoms. The results were in from the good doctor, and I had everything from cancer to smallpox. The next day I was working out of our Andover office. I had promised Charlotte that if I was feeling bad, I would come home. I expected a call from my doctor with some results and to be honest I would prefer not to be in the house when he called.

Work was the usual. People were winding down way too early for the Christmas break. There was a buffet at lunchtime and a load of Christmas games. Tomorrow would be the last time we were all in the office together before everyone disappeared back to their part of the UK to see the year out. Everyone was having a great time, but it was hard for me to get into the festive spirit. I was constantly looking at my phone checking for a call – it was miserable. I left early, making some excuse about having to pop into one of our sites on the way home.

The drive back to Portsmouth gave me time to reason. I thought if I was really ill the doctor would have called already. This gave my overactive mind a rest and I managed to relax for the night. Charlotte had made a nice meal and got a bottle of wine to take my mind off waiting. It worked until I got into bed and my brain was stuck on a loop, thinking the worst.

The next day was our team's Christmas meal in Salisbury. We spent the morning in the office. At lunchtime the team made the executive decision to finish the day at the pub before the evening meal. I wasn't drinking; unfortunately I had to drive back to Portsmouth that night, although I did have a cheeky pint to wet the whistle. In the pub my line manager at the time came over and sat with me. He asked if I was okay; he recognised I hadn't been myself for a few days.

That was a shock to me because I thought I had been hiding my worry well. I had that funny feeling again when being asked questions like this, as if I was sitting in front of a headmaster and explaining myself. I know he was genuinely concerned for me and not just worried about my work performance, or he would have talked to me in the office. I felt awkward but unloaded everything on him. I told him about all the symptoms I was having and how it was preying on my mind. He was really good and tried his best to make me feel better and offered me as much support as he could in line with his contractual obligations. I felt better getting it off my chest and if he knew something was up with me then the rest of the team must have sniffed it out also.

It was time to move on to the Giggling Squid for our Christmas meal with an Asian twist. More of the team met us at the restaurant: we had the place packed out. It was great to see so many people having a good time. I let go of my worries for a while and joined in with some of the games floating around – there were some rude word-association games going on. Then the food started to arrive. Everyone settled down and began to swap funny work stories as people do in these situations.

By chance I got my phone out. I had a missed call from my doctor's surgery – I still had my phone on bloody silent from being in the office that morning. They hadn't left a message. It was 6pm so I chanced it. I apprehensively popped outside and shakily pressed the call back. The reception lines were closed. This came as an unexpected relief to me. I went back in the restaurant and placed my phone on the table so I could keep an eye on it. I didn't expect a call back so late, but it didn't stop me hovering over my phone like a hawk.

Not 20 minutes later, while I was enthralling my work colleagues with my witty banter and dazzling repartee, my phone started to ring. There in bold across the screen, Bosmere Medical Practice. My heart sank. I didn't want to answer. I had the same feeling you get after a job interview, when you get the call to inform you of your fate. Cutting my conversation short, I picked up the phone and rushed out into the cool December air. I knew deep down that it wasn't going to be good if they were ringing me this late in the evening.

My voice cracked as I answered the phone. On the other end a doctor I had not met before introduced himself. He asked me some confirmation questions to verify who I was. His next question was whether I could get to the surgery before 7pm 'to pick up my prescription'. I was confused and asked, 'What prescription?' He asked me if I had been to the hospital today. 'No,' I said. 'Oh,' he replied. His end went quiet for what seemed like ages. He asked if I had talked to anyone at all today. NO! Fear was setting in, and I was getting frustrated.

He was skirting around something. I asked him outright what was going on. He said that I had a heart condition and that some medication had been prescribed to me. He said I needed to start taking it as soon as possible. I couldn't believe what he was telling me, a heart condition? Had I been to the hospital? What the bloody hell was going on? He asked if I could get to the surgery before 7pm and he would talk me through it. If not, he would place my prescription with the pharmacy next door for me to collect and I could come in first thing in the morning.

I was so angry – something was going on and he wasn't telling me. Some communication had slipped up somewhere. Doctors were making decisions behind the scenes without telling me. There was no chance of me getting to the surgery. It was over an hour back to Havant and it was now 6.20pm already. I walked into the restaurant, gave my line manager some cash, and left without finishing my meal or saying goodbye. My workmates were just staring at me as I left. I didn't care. Their thoughts had become the last thing I was worried about. I knew I wouldn't get back by 7pm but that wasn't going to stop me trying.

I rushed out of the restaurant. I ran across what felt like the whole of Salisbury to where my car was parked. I was dodging Christmas revellers and young couples out for walkies with their little yappy dogs. I must have bumped into three or four different people in my efforts to get to my car. Now significantly sweaty with my Christmas jumper and big winter coat on, I jumped in the car. I think that run to the car must have been at least 2km. If I had been in a better frame of mind I could have started my Garmin: that 2km was bound to have been a PB.

I sped out of the car park, almost hitting a parked taxi. I had to take it easy through the city but as soon as I was away from people, I drove like a madman. I got on the motorway and my average speed must have been ridiculous. I didn't care if I got pulled over; I wanted to get to that doctor. Inevitably, when the clock hit 7pm I was still on the motorway with miles still to go. I didn't stop or slow down; I still had hope I would catch the doctor before he left for the night. I pulled up in the surgery car park and the only lights on were in the pharmacy next door. I had got there a good 20 minutes late. It was a good effort, though – I must have broken some sort of record getting from Salisbury to Havant as fast as I did.

I had a quick look around the surgery building in the hope that the doc would still be working in an office. I was kidding myself: he would have already been in a trendy wine bar by now. Also, my car was the only one in the car park. Disappointment bordering on despair washed over me, the worst-case scenarios running through my head. I tried to steady my beating heart and take a few breaths before walking into the pharmacy.

Out of breath through worry not exertion, I explained the phone call I had from the doctor. The pharmacist knew exactly who I was and asked me to sit in a waiting area. A few moments later he appeared with a big white bag. This wasn't just one item of medication, this was a bag full of them. I demanded to know from the poor pharmacist what was going on. He explained calmly that he didn't know my diagnosis. He told me how to take the medication and when, but I was not taking in anything he was now saying, because he couldn't answer what I wanted to know. I sat there nodding yes, just so I could get out of there and get home. He handed the bag over and inside were four items of medication, Ramipril among others. Back in the car I looked through the bag, scared to death knowing that I had a heart issue, but not knowing what or how bad.

I returned home and Charlotte's face was a mask of puzzlement. 'What are you doing home?' she asked. I wasn't due back until around 11.30pm. She knew I wouldn't be drinking but I had planned to see the night out. I wanted to see if my colleagues did anything daft while drunk. I explained the whole fiasco of the phone call, heart issues, speeding back to Havant and finally the pharmacist. Charlotte couldn't believe that I had been given meds without knowing what for.

We called 111 to see if there was anything we could do that night. They were sympathetic but advised me to call the GP surgery in the morning. Stupidly we then did the worst thing possible. We started to google the medication. The conditions coming back were heart attack, heart disease, diabetes, some forms of cancer. You can safely say I was now experiencing a mixture of emotions: first, I was shitting myself and second, I was angry that no one had talked to me about what was wrong.

Trying to sleep was hopeless. I ended up going back downstairs, blankly watching the pictures moving across the TV screen like a zombie. I realise now I was in some form of shock. I must have sat there like that for hours. When I next looked at my phone it was 3am. I dragged myself to bed and dozed on and off until Charlotte got up for work. I don't know if it was my state of mind, but I lay there pretending to sleep until everyone had left the house for school and work.

When I was sure I was alone in the house I got up and rang my line manager and told him I was sick, and I wouldn't be online today. He was pretty cool about it, as I think he was possibly still drunk from the Christmas meal. I am sure there wasn't that much working from home that day; most of the other guys would be travelling across the country to get home. So there was no guilt from my end. I prepared myself to start making phone calls left, right and centre and demand answers.

I rang my doctor's surgery first; I got through to the stuffy receptionist and explained my story. I wasn't sure she was even listening because she told me all the appointments were taken for the morning and to call back at 1.30pm. I lost my cool and demanded that she confirm she had heard what I was saying. I spelt it out for her again, 'THE DOCTOR TOLD ME TO COME IN THIS MORNING!' She said there was nothing on my notes about this. She went away and a few minutes later she returned with a new attitude: 'Mr Conway, the doctor would be delighted to see you at 1pm. Sorry for any confusion.' Score!

Appointment acquired, now to have a coffee and some toast. Just then my phone started to ring. It was a withheld number. Half expecting it to be work or a sales call, I answered. It was the cardiology department of the Queen Alexandra Hospital in Portsmouth, telling me an appointment had been made for me at 11am. I agreed I would be there. Now I had two appointments. I thought about cancelling the GP appointment, but I kept it just in case.

I arrived at the hospital around 40 minutes early. I had nothing better to do, so took a slow drive there. I didn't ring Charlotte or tell anyone I was going. I didn't even think of telling anyone. I grabbed a coffee and sat waiting for an appropriate time. I watched people wander in and out of the hospital, trying to guess if they were happy or sad. Had they got good news or bad news? Hospitals can be scary places: sometimes people go in and never come out. I was scared. I walked up the stairs to Level C and made my way to the department's reception desk.

I was asked for an appointment letter which I didn't have. I must have been super-sensitive, but this receptionist was treating me the same as the GP's receptionist. 'Sorry sir, if you have an appointment, you would have received a letter.'

'For Christ's sake, you rang me to say I had an emergency appointment.' She went into a little room behind reception and came back with a new attitude, just like the other one, and apologised for any confusion. She said I would first have an ECG and then be called through to the consultant. It was standard procedure ECG, top off, sticky pads everywhere and linked up to loads of cables. The nurse took the readings and said the consultant would have a look at the results before calling me in. I was sent back out with all the other patients to sit in the waiting room. I sized them up. I looked fitter and in better health than most of the other people. I was by far the youngest in there. How bad could this really be?

'Mr Conway,' she called, which snapped me out of my daydream. I walked into a small office with a female consultant. She explained who she was and that she wanted to ask me some questions. I asked her what was wrong with me, and she assured me we would get there. The questions ranged through lifestyle questions, family history questions, exercise questions. We moved on to my symptoms: How long? When did I first notice them? Had I actually passed out when standing up? I answered them all. She asked me to hold on as she needed to speak to someone else.

As I sat there, I noticed a pattern that made me laugh. Nearly every person I had talked to or seen had to talk to someone else and get back to me. They generally come back with a different attitude and an apology. I hope she didn't come back with a new attitude because she was nice. While she was out I tried to look at the notes she had been making while we talked but I couldn't make head nor tail of them. I reached out to flip the notebook around and just as I did, the door handle creaked and in walked a man followed by the female consultant.

My heart sank: I was caught red-handed. The new man didn't seem to notice but the consultant did. She was kind enough not to say anything. The man introduced himself as a professor and asked if I had anyone with me. Alarm bells started to ring. Nope, I hadn't even thought to tell anyone I was coming.

He started to talk; he told me that what he was about to say was important and he would like me to feel free to stop him at any point and ask questions. He also told me to share any feelings I might have. I had two feelings at that point: shitting myself and 'Hurry up and tell me.' He went on in a slow and sympathetic tone. He had reviewed my test results, and I had a condition called heart failure. He explained that my heart wasn't pumping blood efficiently around my body and head. This was causing all my symptoms.

He explained that they didn't know my prognosis or the cause. Shock set in and my mind went to worst possible case scenario. He went on to talk about my pump fraction being low and my aorta being dilated, but I couldn't take any of it in. I wished Charlotte had been with me, she would have taken it all in. I remember him telling me it was serious but manageable and we would manage it together. He did a good job of trying to reassure me that people could live full, active lives with the right treatment.

He said he would stop talking now as I probably had loads of questions. I felt bad and apologised; my mind was blank, empty: I had none. I was in shock and couldn't think of a single thing to ask. He recognised this, leant forward and touched my arm. He said: 'Normally people ask things like: "How long will I live?" At this moment we don't know. We have to get the medication right to see how your heart reacts and how much, if any, your function improves.' He said a few more things but I was gone, I had stopped listening. I felt I had been handed a death sentence.

I have recently talked to a professional about everything and they noted that on multiple occasions, I have shut down and not been able to listen. They explained that it's a natural response to trauma. I couldn't take anything in because my brain was trying to protect me.

The professor moved on to next steps – he informed me that I would be in and out of hospital over the next couple of weeks for tests. He said it was unusual for a person of my age to have this, and he personally would be taking over my care. 'Over the next few weeks, we will optimise your meds to reduce the workload on your heart.' I was to monitor my salt and fluid intake. Normally he would recommend that a person do light exercise but, in my case, I was to stop for a while and let my heart rest.

I was given a load of leaflets and told what emergency signs to look for. He told me that he would now send me for some more tests and then book me in to see him in the next few days. I was then taken to get some blood tests and an echocardiogram. I had to get a massive jug that contained acid. I was told that for the next 24 hours I was to put all my urine in this jug. It was explained to me that I did not want to get any of the acid in the jug on my penis as it would burn it off. Then they let me go. I ended up weeing in one of Charlotte's mixing jugs. I chucked it away after.

I got in the car and sat there for a good half an hour trying to take it all in. I first felt numbness when the good professor was talking to me. I had become strangely detached, as if he hadn't been talking about me. Then the diagnosis settled over me like a fog. The words 'heart failure' carried the weight of a death sentence; fear that had crept in during the day was now shouting in my head. I cried in the car. I thought about not having a future: would I see the kids finish school, get jobs and marry? Would I see my next birthday? Would this be my last Christmas?

I allowed myself this time to get as much emotion out of my system as possible. I had the hardest job to do next. I had to go home and tell Charlotte. How do you say something like that? The words felt like stones in my throat, too heavy and jagged to get out. I practised over and over in my head what I was going to say. I couldn't find the right words to soften the blow.

'The doctor said my heart isn't working as well as it should'? Nope, that was too vague and she would find out when she came to the next set of appointments. 'I don't know how much time I have left'? Nope, that was too brutal. I would just tell her, 'heart failure' and play it down, try not to upset her too much. It's crazy what goes through your head. Here I was, having just been told something was terribly wrong with me, and I was now more worried about how Charlotte was going to react. I got home and sat waiting for Charlotte, so I could break the news.

When Charlotte arrived home, she was in a chipper mood. I felt bad that I had to stop that. I told her to sit, and she saw all the paperwork I had been given, including the massive urine jug which now had two or three of my contributions sloshing around in it. I took her hand and told her the truth. I told her what I remembered the doctors saying. I told her about all the symptoms I had been having for a long time. She cried and I hugged her, and I felt I had to swallow my fear, because in that moment hers was louder. I realised that telling her was actually easy, but the selfish thing that made it difficult was that now I had to live with her grief as well as mine.

The next few days were spent going in and out of hospital for tests and bloods and more questions. I felt like a ghost, half in this new world of being sick, and half in the world I had lived in before I found out. People didn't know what was going on and we pretended that nothing was wrong. One appointment blended into the next. Luckily Charlotte was keeping track, as I was content to float through it all like the ghost I felt. It was almost Christmas, so I didn't want to tell anyone and spoil it. Only Charlotte and I knew. Again, that selfish feeling. I didn't want to deal with anyone else's grief or worry – I had my own to deal with.

The doctors couldn't figure out what had caused my heart failure. There were a number of theories: I had a genetic problem that caused the damage; at some point I might have had a heart infection that had caused the damage; they even looked at the possibility of COVID jabs causing it.

They booked me an appointment for a cardiac MRI at St Thomas and Guy's Hospital in London in the New Year and I was told to enjoy Christmas as much as I could and they would see me in January. I went a little over the top trying to enjoy Christmas: I bought expensive food and alcohol and extra presents for the kids. It seemed to be a strange duality: outwardly I was trying to enjoy Christmas but, in the background, I was preparing for death. I created a folder for Charlotte with all the information she needed if I were to die. I even started to sell stuff I no longer used, to help her financially.

The medications I had been put on were also messing with me physically. My body had not yet adapted to them, and I was constantly tired and dizzy. The effects of the meds and living two lives, one where I was ill and the other pretending to be okay, sent me into a deep depression. I 100 per cent thought my time was up and I can't explain what effect that has on your mind. I think Charlotte noticed this and pleaded with me that I should tell people what was wrong with me. I said that I would tell Simon and Rob. Simon had only just got back from working overseas and was due to come round ours on New Year's Eve for some drinks.

Unfortunately, Simon's kids were ill so Kayley, his wife, stayed at home with them and only Simon came round. He had brought a few beers, so we cracked one open and Charlotte went upstairs. I let him have it. I told him the whole story. It felt good. Simon didn't act emotionally, which I knew I needed. He acted clinically and in an ordered fashion. He asked specific questions about my heart and next steps. Then he said we should celebrate, which I thought was strange.

It was still early, and he got me in the car, and we went to the only off-licence we could find open. He bought me a bottle of whisky and himself a bottle of rum. We spent the whole night on my sofa reminiscing about the good old days. He knew exactly what I needed in that moment – no sorrow, no grief, just acceptance of what I was going through and then some normality. The next day, with Simon beside me, we called Rob and told him my news. The next day he was travelling the 200-odd miles in his van to spend some time with me. It was great: we chilled in the house, we went out to the New Year sales, and it took my mind off everything. I will always be grateful for having Simon and Rob; they are in the truest of senses my best friends.

The year had ended badly but at least I now had an answer to all the strange symptoms I was having: dizziness, cold, numb thumbs and hands, the anxiety and fear, were all from my heart not working properly. My heart was causing the anxiety symptoms and when a normal amount of stress was present in me my heart rate would overreact as if I was in a life or death situation. I felt worse when at rest because my heart rate was below 40 beats per minute. The minute I started running or working out I felt better because my heart was working harder and pumping more blood around my body. Now we just had to figure out what had caused it and what my prognosis was.

I attended my cardiac MRI in London, and it was the strangest thing I had been through. I was connected up to a plastic IV and pumped with a fluid that made my arm and body go cold. I was in a big noisy tube. In the headphones placed over my ears I would be told when to breathe in and out and when not to fill my lungs. It was difficult to do and a few times I was straining for breath.

We were called back to our local hospital for the results of the MRI, and we had good news – my pump fraction had increased but not back to normal range. It had gone in the right direction. Normally I would have been discharged to a community heart-failure nurse but due to my age and how unusual it is for someone my age to have this condition, I stayed under the care of the professor.

As I write this in 2025, it has been over two years since diagnosis, and we are still no closer to understanding what caused this issue. In those two years all has not been plain sailing; on occasions my heart pump function has gone in the wrong direction. I have become more tired and often go to bed at 7pm after work as I am that exhausted.

I was once asked by a tipsy friend at a party what it felt like to go through this and have it on my mind for the last few years. The first year was denial wrapped in hope. My heart improved, which gave me hope and I thought the doctors were wrong, but then it went backwards again. I followed the prescribed medication routine and the diet, and the advice given by the cardiologists, GPs and heart failure nurses, who all talk in percentages and ejection fractions.

In my head I would tell myself just to do everything right and I could outrun this. But I couldn't; the tiredness and fatigue it caused felt like a lead blanket pulling me down to the ground. Even the willpower I had to run ultra marathons and box in a ring wasn't enough to lift that heavy blanket off my back. I cancelled plans, I took naps in my car while on my break at work and I learned to smile and nod at the 'You look tired' comments. What I feared the most was becoming that 24-stone man again; I couldn't train at anywhere near the level and intensity that I used to and this preyed on my mind daily.

The second year I lost that hope and the ache of acceptance set in. The condition became a part of me, no longer something I had. The grim routine of multiple medications every day and appointments with the hospital, my GP and special appointments with a pharmacist all became normal. I gained a dark humour about my mortality and started to play on it with Charlotte: 'I couldn't possibly do the dishes – I have a weak heart!'

Mentally I was split in two. One person obsessively tracked my symptoms like a mad scientist who clutches at hope and celebrates after a good check-up or minuscule improvement. Then there was my shadow self that whispered in my ear, 'This is how it ends, what's the point in starting that project? What's the point in trying that new thing?' These two selves constantly battle: there's no compromise. I am either one or the other, no blend or mix.

With time things got better and there are odd moments where I forget, the luminous rare moments. For me these moments normally come when laughing and joking with Simon and Rob or Scott and Nath, when I lie next to Charlotte in bed and absent-mindedly talk about rubbish.

One good thing heart failure has taught me to understand what is important and what's not. Normally these are little things from work: someone missing a deadline, or an employee bad-mouthing you because you're the boss. I now think these things are unimportant and they don't affect me. In general, my condition has forced me to be more stoical. If not, I would have given up by now.

Chapter 16

Where Am I Now?

IT'S BEEN over three years since the diagnosis, and my heart health fluctuates between appointments. I have regular check-ups and sometimes I leave positive and sometimes it's all doom and gloom. I have had to learn that heart failure can fluctuate even on a daily basis.

It can drive you mad because it leaves you thinking, 'What was I doing right when my test results showed improvements?' Had I relaxed more? Had I eaten less sugar? It's frustrating not to be in total control of your own body.

Some days I feel low and fatigued, and I just want to hide away to be left alone. On good days, I feel fantastic. I feel like my old ultra-running self again. At the moment, these days are pretty even, but I know they will get worse over time. I have to be careful when I'm ill with a normal cold because my heart can beat harder, and I can feel every beat.

WHERE AM I NOW?

It doesn't just affect you physically but also mentally. It drives me mad. My mind is willing and wants me to run and box, but my body won't allow me to. Over time, the fear of dying has slipped away, and this has been replaced by a new fear. To me a worse fear than dying is going back to 24-stone man. I have put a couple of stone back on due to having to cut my physical exercise to a minimum, and that terrifies me.

Recently, having talked more openly with my consultant and discussed my fears and how my condition affects my mental health, I have been given a green light to increase my training load. I have had to start at a very low intensity, not allowing my heart rate to go anywhere near its maximum. I follow the guidance of my consultant to go low and slow. Any irregular feelings or skipped beats, then I stop. I follow this guidance religiously. I run a little and then walk so that my heart rate drops, then I repeat this for a couple of kilometres.

I then go back to the hospital after a month or so and check to see if I have had any adverse effects from stepping up my exercise. I have had mainly positive effects on my mental health because I am doing something. However, I'm still frustrated as there don't seem to be any positive physical effects, although it hasn't had any negative physical effects. This has led to my consultant allowing me to add more intensity to my exercise. I can up the heart rate a little more.

This step up has been a godsend. I treated myself to a nice new, shiny red Scott road bike. I find that I can cycle, keeping a relative low heart rate and get some good distances going.

I'm now more confident that my heart isn't going to stop, which was always at the back of my mind. I have begun to push the boundaries that the consultant had set for me. I let my heart rate rise above my set limit and then let it come back down. I have started to be bolder and hit 50–60km on a single ride again. I know it's naughty, but I feel good. In my mind, it's no different to when Coach Dave would tell me to slow down and not go too hard.

During a recent appointment, I tentatively showed the consultant my Garmin bike data. He went quiet and furrowed his brow. He sat back in his chair and scrolled through the data on my phone. Instantly I thought, 'He's going to bollock me.' He placed the phone on his desk, looked me in the eye, and asked if I had really been cycling those distances. Yes, I told him. He then went into a flurry of questions about how I felt during and after the bike rides. I told him: 'Absolutely fine, sometimes I get tired, but no major heart attacks, no heart stoppages, and no dying.'

He didn't bollock me at all. He was genuinely pleased for me. While he was happy and I had shown I was a little more capable than he might have thought, I took my chance and slyly asked if I could step up the distance I had shown him. He eagerly said, 'Of course,' before checking himself and quizzically asking what to.

I told him, '100km – I want to do the New Forest 100km again.'

In a flat and emotionless tone, he asked, 'Do you think you can do it?'

'YES!' I replied.

From that point on, he was on board. He told me to take it easy, and if I had any problems, I was to stop and phone an ambulance. I promised him that I would. When I left the hospital, the air smelled a little fresher and I felt excited again. I felt like I was back. The nerdy thing I was most looking forward to was the planning of the training, the researching of the route, everything that was involved in getting to an event like a 100km bike ride.

That's what I did. I planned my training to a tee. I wasn't aiming to break any speed records. It would be a nice leisurely 100km: the distance was the target, not the time. I obsessively checked my cycling and heart stats, blood pressure, BPM, blood oxygen, and everything was lining up nicely.

The day of the ride came around and I woke up early, had the old go-to breakfast of peanut butter on toast, and it tasted so much better knowing it was going to be used as fuel. I got to the race event with a mixture of excitement and trepidation. The people and bikes all getting ready to achieve the same goal of finishing the event and getting that little bit of metal to go around your neck gave me goosebumps.

I also had a sickly stomach knot because, no matter how much prep I had done or training, my heart was knackered, and that preyed on my mind: would I be able to finish the ride? Would I make anything worse? Yes, it felt good to be back, but I was worried. I kept to myself, prepped my bike and sipped some water. I was sitting on a grass verge with my back against a fence, letting the sun warm my face.

The time was nigh, so I moved to the start line. For me, this event felt more momentous than my first ultra marathon. I thought it best not to be anywhere near the front in the mix with the Lycra Lance Armstrongs. I don't want to get too competitive and have a heart attack trying to keep up with them. The person starting the race was saying something on a megaphone, but I already had my headphones in, listening to some lo-fi hip-hop beats to keep me relaxed. Bad form, I know.

She set us off, and away we went. I started off slow and steady, keeping the distance in mind, not speed.

WHERE AM I NOW?

The first 50–60km went well, no issues at all. I was drinking nicely and eating every now and then. When I got to untested territory – untested now I had heart failure – I got in my own mind and began worrying what might happen to my heart. I then started worrying about worrying!

At 70km it was too much, and I stopped for an extended break after an aid station. I found myself a nice patch of grass that overlooked a few fields and lay down in the sun. I may have looked like a serene cyclist catching a few rays, but in my head was a battle not to give up and call the sad old car that sweeps up the stragglers at the end of a race.

I couldn't help but be terrified of making things worse, but another side of me was arguing that if it was that bad, the consultant would have told me there was no chance. After 20 minutes, I hopped back on the bike and pedalled on through the worry. With 10km to go, I was blowing out of my arse. I am ashamed to say I had to jump off the bike and walk it up a hill, something I had never done before.

It was the slowest 10km ever. I think I was overtaken by everyone left in the race. When I finally managed to get across the finish line, I knew I must have been one of the last because the place was dead. There were not many people left at all. I didn't feel much emotion crossing the line. Physically, my lungs were on fire, my legs were trembling with fatigue, and all I wanted was to get home and in the bath.

I collected my medal and freebies and chucked everything in the car. I did my checks and measured my blood pressure, pulse rate and blood oxygen. It must have been weird for anyone to see a sweaty bloke sitting in his car testing himself with medical equipment. Everything was in order. It was only on the drive home that I became emotional, somewhere around Southampton. You may think it was because I was now a die-hard supporter of Portsmouth Football Club and I was driving past the old enemy. No, the previous time I had driven this way was the night I had had to speed from my Christmas meal in Salisbury to pick up some medication with no explanation.

At the time I had heart failure and not known. I had an overwhelming sense of pride and vindication, remembering all those hospital visits when I wondered if I could ever get back to exercise – and here I was now doing it, albeit a lot more slowly. It certainly gave me a confidence boost and allowed me to understand what my body and heart were capable of.

This, of course, was actually the second time for me learning what my body could do. The first time was understanding that my 24-stone frame was capable of transformation into that of an ultra-runner and boxer. The second time was learning what I could do without making my heart worse. I often think that if I hadn't driven along the M27 towards Portsmouth that day, and remembered the last time I had driven that way, would I have experienced any emotion, would I have felt proud? Or rather than delayed-onset muscle soreness, had I simply got delayed-onset emotional feelings?

I look at that ride now as a symbol. For me it was a middle finger to heart failure and a love letter to resilience. Even a broken body can surprise you. It was certainly a confidence booster.

As the winter came around, I put the bike away and joined a little gym just a few minutes' walk from my house. The gym was small and had one of everything. I was going in at six in the morning and completing around 20 minutes of cardio and then 40 minutes of weights. Every morning I had the gym to myself. Not another soul would enter the place at that time. It was fantastic to start my days that way. It would set me up for a hard day's work. The more and more I went to the gym, the more and more I was using the treadmill. I was getting the running bug back. The 20 minutes of cardio slowly increased to 40 on the treadmill and 30 minutes of weights.

This leads me nicely up to the present. It's now summer 2025 and I have exchanged my 6am gym sessions for a 6am running club. I am still finding running difficult. Some mornings I struggle with breathing and some days my legs are dead weight. But I am now running for the joy of running.

Of course, I would love to hit some bigger distances, but I am loving running alongside Langstone Harbour as the sun rises and I feel its warm rays on my face – until winter, when it will be cold and dark and I will be back in the gym. I am now up to running 6km non-stop, albeit slowly. The other day I did 5km in 30 minutes. I hadn't done that in years.

My main ambition now is to lose the two stone I have put back on since diagnosis. I am also allowing myself the dream of completing the Great South Run again at some point. I would love to get back to the level where a 10-mile run is no problem again. It would be great to run it for the British Heart Foundation, or a great heart failure charity called Pumping Marvellous. It would give me something to aim for again, or as Charlotte would say, something to obsess over again.

At some point, heart failure will catch up with me, and I won't be able to run anymore, but while I am running, there's still a gap between us.

Acknowledgements

IT'S BEEN a proper old journey writing this book and I have come to realise that there have been many people that have helped and supported me along the way. My biggest thanks go to my ever-suffering wife, Charlotte. I know I am not easy to live with sometimes, and you are a saint for putting up with me – everyone says so!

Thanks to my children, Chloe and Archie, for supporting me. A big thanks to Dave Butters (Coach Dave) for helping me to achieve my goals. Thanks to Dave McBride (Work Dave) and Charlotte Morrison for supporting me at the beginning of this journey. Thanks to my mates Simon Sims and Rob Box for forever shining light in the dark. And thanks to Scott Griffiths and Nathan Ware for always being there with the pints. Thanks also to Amber Page for looking over my work and correcting my bad English.

There are so many others to thank but I have a word limit to achieve: you know who you are.

And finally, thank you to all that have read this. I hope it's helped.